TALLGRASS PRAIRIE

Text by John Madson
Photographs by Frank Oberle

The
Nature
Conservancy®

BOOKS FOR
CONSERVATION

FALCON
PRESS®

Helena, Montana

To Sy Runkel
and his ageless, unfailing sense of wonder

Published in cooperation with The Nature Conservancy.

The author gratefully acknowledges permission to adapt portions of
the chapter "On The Osage" from *Nature Conservancy* magazine, and
to adapt portions of "A Place Of Hope And Promise" from *National
Wildlife Magazine*.

Editing, design, typesetting, and other prepress work
by Falcon Press, Helena, Montana.
Binding and printing in Korea.

Library of Congress Number 93-25835

ISBN 1-56044-223-9

For extra copies of this book please check with your local
bookstore, or write to Falcon Press, P.O. Box 1718, Helena,
MT 59624. You also may call toll-free 1-800-582-2665.

Madson, John.
    Tall grass prairie / John Madson ; photos by Frank Oberle.
       p. cm.
    ISBN 1-56044-223-9
    1. Prairies--Middle West. 2. Prairie ecology--Middle West.
    3. Prairies--Middle West--Pictorial works. 4. Prairie ecology-
    -Middle West--Pictorial works.   I. Oberle, Frank. II. Title.
QH104.5M47M34 1993
574.5'2643'0973--dc20   93-25835
                                                                CIP

Contents

TALLGRASS PRAIRIE

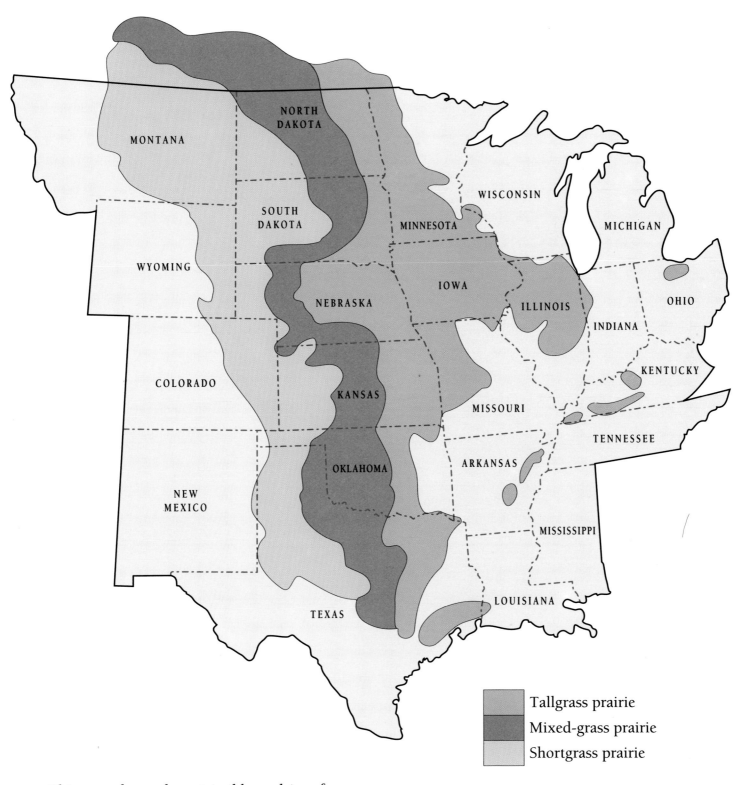

This map shows the original boundries of
tallgrass, mixed-grass, and shortgrass prairies that
once spanned much of mid-America. Today only
small remnants of the tallgrass prairie remain
unplowed or undeveloped.

FOREWORD

What is it about prairies? What fascinates us so about the grasslands that gird our continent?

Other landscapes, certainly, offer more obviously spectacular scenery. The soaring peaks of the Rockies, the fabulous redrock formations of the Southwestern deserts, sweeping ocean coastlines—these are the picture-postcard images that we conjure up when we think of the beauty of our natural heritage.

By contrast, the prairie seems, well, flat—flat and somewhat monotonous, undeniably vast but not as picturesque as a redwood forest or a mountain stream.

Yet the prairie holds a rightful place in American popular culture as one of our most distinctive and defining landscapes. Writers from Washington Irving to Willa Cather to Carl Sandburg have celebrated the prairie in prose and verse. Our national songs refer to the "endless prairie" and "the fruited plain." Illinois, where only one-hundredth of one percent of its original grassland remains intact today, proudly calls itself the Prairie State.

I think that no single factor can explain the power of the prairie and its lasting grip on the American imagination. Part of it, no doubt, stems from the role that the prairie has played in our history. The dramas of settler and Native American were played out on the prairie. It gave us Buffalo Bill, prairie schooners, and prairie populists. The great cattle drives of the 19th century crossed this landscape. And the prairie effortlessly swallowed up tens of thousands of homesteaders, each staking out their claim to a quarter-section.

The prairie also stands as an enduring reminder of our country's immense natural resources. These days, most people see the prairie from the air, and what they see are orderly farm fields marching unbroken from horizon to horizon. No matter that much of the original prairie has been plowed under to make way for row crops; no matter that cattle have replaced the bison as the primary grazers. To many people, the prairie represents America's breadbasket, the richness and fertility of the land.

In early summer, prairie phlox and Indian paintbrush rise from the tall grasses that will soon engulf them at Coyne Prairie, Missouri.

And perhaps most of all, the prairie serves as a symbol of the frontier: an idealized vision of a landscape as perfectly empty and impressive as it was when the first settlers pushed their way out of the great Eastern forest and onto the plains. The prairie is the land of the spacious skies and open vistas. Just knowing it is there comforts those of us who live on the heavily populated coasts.

But for me, the power of the prairie is far more subtle. It must be experienced up close. Walking on the prairie opens up a magical world that cannot be replicated by riding in an airplane or driving on an interstate highway.

For one, the burning in your calves will soon remind you that the prairie is not flat. Rather, the prairie rises and falls in long swells like a grass ocean. Hidden within the folds of this deceptive terrain lie small pools of water (the so-called "prairie potholes"), ravines thick with post oak, blackjack, and cottonwoods, and clumps of rock left by retreating glaciers long ago.

The prairie also teems with the signs of animal life, past and present. Curious depressions in the ground, for example, provide evidence of a buffalo wallow of

old. On every fencepost, it seems, sits a hawk; raptors and buteos circle in the skies. Walk across the prairie and you'll invariably flush a brace of prairie chickens or a covey of quail. If you're fortunate, perhaps you'll even find the tracks of a bobcat.

When you walk on the prairie, you also learn that the grasses are not uniform, not by any means. In fact, the most startling thing about the prairie might well be the immense diversity of plant life that it harbors. At The Nature Conservancy's Tallgrass Prairie Preserve in

Left: The katydid has taken on the color of the purple poppy mallow it is eating.

the Osage Hills of Oklahoma, for example, botanists have identified more than 500 different species of plants without trying very hard.

The namesake tallgrasses, of course, are there in abundance—big bluestem, Indian grass, cord grass. But interspersed thickly amid these majestic grasses are hundreds of other plants, such species as the little bluestem, prairie dropseed, needlegrass, sideoats grama, and the compass plant, as tasty as ice cream for a hungry cow or bison.

And then there are the flowers. As John Madson writes, "From the first pasqueflowers of March to the towering sunflowers of October, the tallgrass prairie will never be without flowers." To walk waist-deep in prairie flowers is to stroll through a fragile and fragrant world unlike any other.

———

Thanks to this book, you don't have to walk the prairie to appreciate the wonder of this distinctive American landscape. John Madson and Frank Oberle have collaborated to celebrate the prairie in words and images worthy of the subject.

Madson, a long-time contributor to *Nature Conservancy* magazine, has prepared a text as deceivingly simple and beautiful as the prairie. Drawing on sources from Pere Marquette—one of the first Europeans to encounter the prairie—to Aldo Leopold, he weaves an engaging, informative, and highly personal tale about the natural history of the landscape. This is nature writing at its finest, a tribute to the prairie that is and a eulogy to the prairie that is lost.

Perfectly complementing Madson's text are the stunning photographs of Frank Oberle, also a regular contributor to the Conservancy's magazine. Gleaned from more than 3,000 rolls of film, these pictures—works of art, really—document the diversity and visual power of the prairie. They distill the experience of thousands of hours of exploring the prairie into beautiful and accessible images.

Readers of this book should also know these images reflect a true labor of love. For Frank Oberle is

A prairie white-fringed orchid, a threatened species.

Above: A cardinal flower peeks through prairie sedges at The Nature Conservancy's Wah-sha-she ("the water people") Prairie in southwestern Missouri.

Left: White lady slipper orchids and yellow stargrass bloom in early May at The Nature Conservancy's Hoffman Prairie, Iowa.

nothing if not dedicated. He has become a well-known character on Nature Conservancy preserves across the prairie belt, following the explosion of spring flowers from south to north with the relentlessness of a bloodhound on a fresh trail. John Madson says that Oberle traveled 65,000 miles to gather these photographs, but I suspect the total to be far greater.

The Nature Conservancy is proud of its association with these two artists. We are proud also of our efforts to preserve prairies across the United States. From the Niobrara Valley Preserve in the Sand Hills of Nebraska to the Konza Prairie in Kansas to our showpiece Tallgrass Prairie Preserve in Oklahoma, the Conservancy has set aside some of the best remaining examples of prairie in the United States.

You can walk these prairies, as I have, and experience the world as it once was. Or you can let John Madson and Frank Oberle take you there. Or best of all, try to do both. Your appreciation for the prairie—and for this fine book—will surely grow.

JOHN C. SAWHILL
President, The Nature Conservancy

A male bobolink sings from its perch on a grass stem at the Conservancy's Kettledrummer Prairie in western Minnesota.

Big bluestem is the signature grass of the true prairie, and its rich, winey color heralds autumn at the Conservancy's Freda Haffner Kettlehole Preserve in northwestern Iowa. Heath aster grows in the foreground.

"Niawathe" means "the life giver" in the Osage Indian language, and in spring and early summer Missouri's Niawathe Prairie gives life to fields of pale purple coneflowers.

INTRODUCTION

The North is too cold, the West too barren, the East too bloody. This place is just right.

Mesquakie Indians (Iowa)

"THIS FRUITFUL CHAMPAYNE COUNTRIE"

Every American has the right as part of his cultural heritage to stand in grass as high

as his head in order to feel some small measure of history coursing his veins

and personally establish an aesthetic bond with the past.

William H. Elder, "Needs and Problems of Grassland Preservation"

Black-robed Jesuits were the first Europeans to see it, and named the place as best they could. *Prérie* was their word for it.

Back in France and parts of Belgium it had meant grassland, a grassy orchard, or perhaps a park with scattered trees. A good word, with the sound of home in it. So when Pére Jacques Marquette emerged from dark northern forests into the sunny, game-rich savannas of the Mississippi valley in 1673, it may have been something like coming home—and he lovingly noted *les belles préries* in his journal.

Pére Claude Jean Allouez retraced Marquette's route down the Illinois River, adding extravagant praise of his own:

We proceeded, always continuing to coast along the great preries, which extend farther than the eye can reach. Trees are met with from time to time, but they are so placed they seem to have been planted with design, in order to make the avenues more pleasing to the eye than those of orchards. The bases of these trees are often watered by little streamlets, at which are seen large herds of stags and hinds refreshing themselves, and peacefully feeding on the short grass....

Left: Coyne Prairie in southwestern Missouri is the rarest of the rare: privately owned prairie that has never been plowed.
Above: A ruby-throated hummingbird feeds on blue false indigo.

Prérie it was then; *prairie* it would become when the word was adopted (somewhat grudgingly) and anglicized by the English. So it has been ever since. There was no better name for the rich grasslands that were first met by those early explorers. But while the word may have had European roots, the place did not, for it was wholly unlike anything the newcomers had ever seen.

As the first English colonists landed on the Atlantic coast, they were surely awed by the wall of ancient forest that rose beyond the tideline. Its magnitude beggared comprehension; its purposes did not. After all, their homes in Britain had never been far from woodlands and even forests; they knew about trees, and the uses to which they could be put. Trees were for hewing and building—and for two hundred years the colonists hewed and built, cleared and sowed, settled and increased, growing in skill as forestland farmers.

As they slowly worked their way westward with a sharpening land-hunger, they began to find that the forestland behind their Atlantic coast was not endless after all. It did not reach unbroken across the new continent to a distant sea. Several hundred miles inland, the ancient fabric of forest began to show rents and gaps. Strange open lands began to appear, places that could not be explained. These were not storm-racked

Right: Sunset fires the sky above pale purple coneflowers at The Nature Conservancy's 32,000-acre Tallgrass Prairie Preserve in Oklahoma.

Wood lilies such as these at Kettledrummer Prairie do grow in open woodland, but they are equally common in tallgrass prairie.

Above: Indian grass is sometimes called "gold plume" for obvious reasons. One of the classic tallgrasses of the true prairie, it is common on the Conservancy's Konza Prairie in the Flint Hills of Kansas.

Right: Make-believe pioneers celebrate Prairie Days at Missouri's Prairie State Park. The 2,678-acre park was purchased by The Nature Conservancy and transferred to the Missouri Department of Natural Resources.

Big bluestem and sumac line a pathway at Five Ridge Prairie in western Iowa's Loess Hills.

clearings where trees had been windthrown as in some New England pineries. There were simply no trees there at all—only meadows of tall grasses and flowers open to sky and sun. The farther one went westward, the broader such "barrens" became until the land finally outran the forest altogether and merged into a world of limitless grass.

It was country that defied the understanding of farmers born to forest soils and timbered horizons. They held this to be poor land, for what else could account for the lack of trees? Moreover, it was a region of heathen excesses: of grasses that towered above a tall man's head, of birds and animals and flowers never beheld by Christian eyes, of treeless skylines and wild swings of weather ranging from the blazing afternoons of midsummer to the howling gales of midwinter. And the winds—those long, unchecked winds that came running out of some far unknown country to impart their motion to the grasses beneath them.

The French may have been the first Europeans to see the tallgrass prairie country, but they would never fully exploit it. They would build the earliest settlements along certain big prairie rivers, trafficking in furs and frontier commerce, and leaving their lyrical place names. It would be the English and Scotch-Irish, the Scandinavians, Germans and others, who would really put down roots into the deep prairie soils.

There were great problems in this transition from forestland to prairie farming, demanding new ways of thinking and living. Familiar ways and scenes had been left behind in the snug valleys of the Wooden Country; the settlers had crossed an institutional fault as traumatic as the climatic fault that separated treeland from grassland. It demanded change in the ways they looked at themselves and dealt with the land. For one thing, it was found that the rich prairie loams tended to clot and jam on the wooden moldboards of plows meant for light forest soils. But when an Illinois blacksmith named John Deere began marketing his polished steel breaking plows in 1837, the prairie sod capitulated.

The pioneering era in the tallgrass prairie was scarcely a blink in history.

By the time of the Civil War the Grand Prairie of

Historically accurate and ecologically necessary: bison on The Nature Conservancy's 7,800-acre Samuel H. Ordway Memorial Prairie Preserve in South Dakota.

northern Illinois was becoming a vast checkerboard of fields and settlements. Waves of settlers were pouring over into prairie Iowa, then up into southern Minnesota, the Dakotas, Nebraska, and into eastern Kansas. By 1900 the vast domain of unbroken tallgrass prairie had been fragmented; all that remained were little islands of the Old Original that had somehow managed to survive the onslaught of settlement. World War I, with its voracious world appetite for grain, finished most of those. The virgin tallgrass prairie, that "fruitful champayne countrie," had simply been too rich to endure.

There is a curious ambivalence in the American character.

It's as if we cannot get on with the exploiting of original things and places swiftly enough; in desperate haste, like children gobbling cake, we plunder the pelf of a continent—the great pineries, the bison herds, redwood forests. Then, when only vestiges remain, we recant. We recall some of the wonder felt when we first beheld such things, sensing that their loss also spells the fading of our old best dreams—of being young and free and eager to seize the Main Chance. We begin seeing the remnants in a new way, as if looking at them for the first time. We suddenly realize that we knew almost nothing about them; they had been nearly destroyed before given a chance to instruct us. And so, on the second time around, we begin to view them with the reverence and sense of worth with which they should have been addressed in the first place.

So it was with the tallgrass prairie.

With time, and their growing rarity, the surviving scraps and fragments of prairie began to be regarded as cultural curios. The curiosity would be refined into disciplined research, with such scientists as Edgar Transeau and John Weaver taking a close look at the true prairie and its causes. There was also a growing literary celebration of prairie by the likes of Hamlin Garland, Willa Cather, Ole Rolvaag, Aldo Leopold, and Donald Culross Peattie. Finally, the great technical advances of the past forty years have allowed prairie scenes to be recorded with new films and steadily improving color reproduction. For the first time the public at large could see the beauty of prairiescapes through the lenses of

Magenta torches of blazing star brighten a misty summer morning at the Missouri Botanical Garden's Prairie Demonstration Area near Gray's Summit.

Home defense on a prairie marsh: nesting red-winged blackbirds don't tolerate intruders—even those as large as egrets.

Left: Tallgrass prairie could be called "Daisyland" for the abundance of such flowers. These purple coneflowers, sunflowers, and the blazing stars in the distance are all members of the daisy family.

Indian paintbrush on Missouri's Mo-Ko ("medicine") Prairie.

A wild prairie at its springtime best—a riot of creamy wild indigo, Indian paintbrush, white and lavender shooting stars, and yellow stargrass at the Sheldon L. Cook Memorial Meadow near Golden City, Missouri.

gifted photographers—none of whom has seen more tallgrass prairie remnants, or recorded them more faithfully, than Frank Oberle. Over 65,000 miles of travel and 3,000 rolls of film have gone into the rich pageant that unfolds in this book.

Today tallgrass prairie preserves exist in all midwestern states (see chapter six). Some are remnants of original prairie; others are largely restorations. It's hard to say what states have the "best" prairie remnants, but Missouri, Iowa, and Minnesota surely head the list in terms of quantity, quality, and diversity of their prairie sites—a position that Illinois and Wisconsin could challenge. However, finding the public prairies in any of those states can be an adventure in itself. Missouri makes it far easier than most states, with its excellent prairie directories. Ideally, a tallgrass prairie site consists of native flowers and grasses displayed in breadth as well as depth. For sheer size, as well as quality, the Konza Prairie in eastern Kansas' Flint Hills is a prime example, as are the Ordway Prairie in north-central South Dakota and the new Tallgrass Prairie Preserve in northeastern Oklahoma.

Some of the flowers, grasses, and open skylines shown here may no longer exist by the time this is read.

But most of these little lane-ends into yesterday are being succored and preserved. To do otherwise is unthinkable in an age when so much old-time grace and meaning is being paved into oblivion.

In late summer height, big bluestem grass towers over schoolchildren at the Missouri Botanical Garden's Prairie Demonstration Area. Some big bluestem culms may reach ten feet in height.

THE OPENING LAND

You must not be in the prairie; but the prairie must be in you.

William A. Quayle, *The Prairie and the Sea*

THE PRAIRIE SAVANNA

Where I grew up the knotted burr oaks stood, their boughs so long they arched

down to the ground again. And it was under these living arches

that my people came driving their wagons.

Donald Culross Peattie, *A Prairie Grove*

Deep prairie and deep forest are natural enemies.

Such grassland can't survive on the sun-starved floor of a heavy forest whose canopy tends to block the flood of light that grasses must have. The forest can't withstand the frequent fires that help maintain the prairie condition. And so the two biomes have fought an age-old war whose front lines advance and retreat according to climatic trends.

The bitterly disputed skirmish line between prairie and forest was often sharply defined; a landlooker might step out of heavy forest, walk a few paces through a brushy shrub zone, and be confronted with open grassland as far as he could see.

But there were vast areas at the eastern edge of the western prairies and the western edge of the eastern forests where armistice was declared and trees and grass coexisted in beautiful parklike savannas that were neither prairie nor forest. Some ecologists today feel it was the dominant ecosystem through large parts of the cornbelt states, and that much of what has been

Left: Old-time prairie was more than grass. There were open savannas—groves of bur oaks and other trees in parklike stands. Above: A rare yellow-fringed orchid.

Snow covers a savanna of the Konza Prairie near Manhattan, Kansas. The limbs of such evenly-spaced savanna oaks are wide-spreading and near the ground. Like the surrounding prairie, these open groves are maintained by fire.

A creekside savanna on the Konza Prairie is a magnet for wildlife. Although far from major rivers, such places may support rookeries of great blue herons.

regarded as "tallgrass prairie" in those states was actually "tallgrass savanna."

They were striking landscapes that no living person has ever really seen.

In the mid-1800s, a winter traveler in southern Michigan rode into such a savanna late on a winter's day. He was probably in no mood to be impressed by any sort of landscape–but he couldn't help effusing over coming into a prairie savanna for the first time:

Lost as I was, I could not help pausing frequently when I struck the first bur-oak opening I had ever seen, to admire its novel beauty. It looked more like a pear orchard than anything else to which I assimilate it–the trees being somewhat of the shape and size of full-grown pear trees, and standing at regular intervals apart from each other on the firm, level soil....Here, too, I first saw deer in herds; and half-frozen and weary as I was, the sight of the spirited creatures, sweeping in troops through interminable groves, where any eye could follow them for miles over the smooth snowy plain, actually warmed and invigorated me, and I could hardly refrain from putting the rowls to my tired horse, and launching after the noble game.

A cardinal decorates a flowering redbud tree at the Tallgrass Prairie Preserve. Although oaks and cottonwoods dominated prairie tree species, smaller trees and shrubs such as redbuds, wild plum, and Osage orange also lined prairie waterways and savannas.

At the edge of an oak savanna in the Tallgrass Prairie Preserve, a white-tailed deer tests the air for scents.

The hardy bur oak that named such parklike "oak openings" was one of the few trees fitted to survive on upland prairie. The tree had a trick of putting down several feet of taproot in its first summer, while sending up a shoot only twelve inches high, and although the young stem might die in subsequent fires, the rootstock went on growing, sometimes forming masses three feet in diameter. This could go on for a century or more, and one noted botanist has said "there is no good reason why they may not be a thousand years old...."

If a stem made it through the first fifteen years, the young tree was on its way. The bark grew thick, corky, and almost fireproof, withstanding the frequent fires that maintained prairie by killing most other woody plants. When wildfires were suppressed by early settlers, the oak openings quickly reverted to brushland and became closed oak forests.

Classic prairie savannas are far rarer than virgin tallgrass prairie. In all of Illinois, for example, only thirteen acres of tallgrass savanna remnants are known to exist, and those are badly degraded. One has been largely restored by Steve Packard of The Nature Conservancy's Illinois office and many volunteers, who burned a Cook County savanna and reseeded it with grasses and forbs that had been choked out by alien second-growth many years ago.

Today, in many mature woodlands that have been forest as long as anyone can remember, there may be a few old, wide-spreading bur oaks with huge lower branches that nearly sweep the ground–trees bred in the open with little competition, the only survivors of what were once prairie savannas.

No prairie tree is tougher and more enduring than the bur oak, a member of the white oak group.
Its corky bark shields it from prairie fire, and its deep tap root saves it from drought.

THE PRAIRIE WORLD

...more than anything else I felt motion in the landscape; in the fresh, easy-blowing morning wind, and in the earth itself, as if the shaggy grass were a sort of loose hide, and underneath it herds of wild buffalo were galloping, galloping....

Willa Cather, My Antonia

THE GOODLY GRASSES

All flesh is grass, and all the goodliness thereof is as the flower of the field....

Isaiah 40:6

Some early landlookers could see little promise in the prairie. Land that couldn't grow trees couldn't be much good for farming.

They overlooked the obvious: that cultivated grains were the analogs of wild prairie grasses. Corn was simply a tall, domesticated grass. Wheat and oats and barley were mid-height domesticated grasses. And both tall and midgrasses thrived on the early prairies. With time, so would the settlers who learned to understand.

Long after the prairie had been converted to rich farmlands, old-timers spun fireside yarns of how it was when they'd come west to "prove up" their claims. Of how they rode through fields of wild grasses so tall that the stems could be tied in knots over the pommel of a saddle; of how they might have to stand in that saddle in order to find cattle that had vanished from sight in the depths of those grasses.

More often than not they were talking about stands of big bluestem grass, *Andropogon gerardi*, named for the bluish-purple of a main stem that might stand nine

Left: A closeup of big bluestem grass shows the bluish tone that named it.
Above: Sloughgrass with swamp milkweed.

A field of prairie dropseed has been winnowed by the wind on the Konza Prairie in Kansas, while a stand of ripening big bluestem dominates higher ground along the skyline.

Buckeye butterflies pause on a grass stem at The Nature Conservancy's Hole-in-the-Mountain Prairie in Minnesota—an area known for several species of rare butterflies.

Right: Niawathe Prairie in southwest Missouri is among the showiest of midwestern prairies and one of the few having the rare royal catchfly, shown here with black-eyed susans.

Wild iris, or "blue flag," accents a stand of grass in a wet swale at the Freda Haffner Kettlehole Preserve in northwest Iowa. "Kettleholes" were formed from huge blocks of ice embedded in glacial debris. When the ice melted, depressions formed and often became shallow ponds.

feet tall. It was also known as "turkey foot" because of its three-branched seed head. This grass was a stamp of authenticity, defining the special community of grasses and flowers that constitutes tallgrass prairie.

Almost identical to big bluestem in size and requirements was Indian grass, *Sorghastrum nutans*, with its single plumelike seedhead and the yellow culm that gave it a common name "gold stem."

Farther downslope, at the edge of wetter ground, was the third tallgrass—the sloughgrass *Spartina pectinata*. It was variously known as "prairie cord grass" because of its tough stems, and "ripgut" because of the finely serrate leaves that have the stiff wire edges of a butcher knife.

Those are the ones that named the tallgrass prairie, but they weren't alone.

Higher up the prairie slope, generally above the big bluestems and Indiangrasses, stood the rich midgrasses: little bluestem, prairie dropseed, porcupine grass, sideoats grama, needlegrass, and many others. All told, the true prairie held about 150 kinds of grasses, although no more than ten were dominant in their special niches.

Tall or short, grasses defined the three major types of our mid-continental grasslands: the true prairie, the mixed-grass prairie, and the shortgrass prairie. Prairie was home to the tallgrasses; mixed-grass prairie was a transition zone in which mid-height grasses began to outrank the tallgrasses; the Great Plains was the realm of short grama grasses and the curly-leafed buffalo grass.

It was the tallgrass prairie and its savannas, however, that was first met by travelers heading west. And in terms of basic fertility—being blessed with more rainfall than the two other main belts of grassland—it would be the most productive. With true prairie put into corn, and the mixed-grass prairie converted to wheatland, they became the world's richest granaries.

It's all a matter of energy conversion.

Each grass stem is a slender antenna that transmits the flood of solar energy into stores of energy deep within the soil. Unlike the miserly forest, prairie does not hoard its energy in woody tissues. Grass grows and dies back annually. The upper parts may be burned,

The grass pink orchid grows in prairie fens, wet prairies, and uplands. The drier the site, the paler the color.

The pasqueflower is one of the earliest prairie blooms, often appearing in March. Five Ridge Preserve near Sioux City, Iowa, has thousands of these hardy symbols of spring.

their component minerals and other nutrients returned to the soil. Certain lower parts—the vast and intricate masses of rootlets—die and rot to build a rich, fluffy humus. The prairie grasses spend themselves freely and annually, forever deepening and fattening soils and recycling stored energy back up into the animal world. Climax prairie is the product bought with such spending, an investment of energy that compounds itself. Each creature of the prairie community, from bison to farmer, shares the dividends of the grass.

There are other dividends as well. None that can be realized at the local grain elevator, maybe, but which pay off in other ways.

Prairie is a restless world in the growing season. There is almost always wind across this grass ocean, stirring waves of green in a tossing panorama that some of us never tire of watching. Stand at the crest of a long prairie swell covered with little bluestem, where the wind is seen not only as motion but as shifting tones of green. Looking downwind, you see only the light green of upper leaf surfaces. Upwind, the ridge is darkened with deeper underleaf tones and shadows. Farther downslope, the tall stems of turkeyfoot and Indian grass are bending and dancing in the embrace of wind; in the wet swales below there is a winnowing of the somber, conifer-green sloughgrasses.

If there's a best time on the prairie, it may come on a late-summer afternoon when the sun's weight is almost unbearable and there is not the slightest stir of air. Then, from out of the west, a weather front. You watch waves of motion running across the wild meadows, driven by what Wallace Stegner called the "grassy, green, exciting wind, with the smell of distance in it." The smell of rainy coolness, too. That blessed rainy coolness.

As grandad would say: "Boy, that'll git it when it's almost gone!"

Nothing is ever wasted on the prairie. This shed deer antler will be eaten by tiny rodents and recycled; the "dead" prairie grass in which it lies will be burned sooner or later, and its minerals returned to the soil.

FLOWERS OF THE FIELD

The flowers appear on the earth; the time of the singing of birds has come....

The Song of Solomon 2:12

The winter wind has lost much of its cutting edge. The blue northers are being succeeded by spring chinooks. The air is softening. Day by lengthening day the sun climbs in renewed vigor and the prairie begins to breathe a rich, loamy sweetness.

A faint wash of green appears on hillsides blackened by autumn fires; in unburned places the grasspoints are emerging from mats of dead litter. The first of the prevernal flowers are arriving on certain ridgetops, heralding spring at last. Brave little flowers, usually only a few inches high: the lavender, tulip-like blossoms of the pasqueflower, and white, woolly mats of prairie cat's-foot. Then, one fine morning, certain prairie slopes look as if patches of sky had fallen there—and you know that the bird's-foot violets have come.

From then until hard frost, there will be no time when the prairiescape is not enameled with flowers of some kind. They come on in waves, their height usually responding to the rising grasses with which they must compete. They appear in bursts of rich floral

Left: A stand of blazing star dominates a portion of Missouri's Niawathe Prairie.
Above: Fringed gentian, Chiwaukee Prairie, Wisconsin.

Above: Wild rose hips and downy gentian, Chiwaukee Prairie, Wisconsin.

Right: The rolling prairiescape of Konza is decked with blazing star and goldenrod in a setting of sideoats grama grass.

Far right: Purple coneflower, or "Black Samson," is of renewed medical interest for its possible relief of flu symptons. It was widely used by Indians and early doctors for treating many illnesses.

successions of indigo, lavender, gold, cream, crimson, white, magenta—floral pigments that echo everything on the artist's palette. From the first pasqueflowers of March to the towering sunflowers of October, the tallgrass prairies will never be without flowers.

Some are as rare and solitary as jewels; others are tall, bold, and strong. Members of most of North America's great floral families are there: the kin of roses, parsleys, lilies, daisies, orchids, peas, snapdragons, mints, buttercups, forget-me-nots, violets, phloxes, primroses, spurges, daffodils, irises, mallows, buckthorns, nightshades, and others.

It's been suggested that prairie "grassland" be called "daisyland," since so much of the prairie's floral roster belongs to that family. In high summer the prairie is a flaming riot of wild daisies: the coneflowers (both yellow and purple), asters, compassplants, bonesets, goldenrods, blazing-stars, rosinweeds, ironweeds, and prairie coreopsis. In some form, wild daisies are as much a part of true prairie as tallgrasses and grasshoppers.

Some of the showiest blooms in these wild gardens are members of the pea family, legumes that help charge the prairie soil with the nitrogen from their root systems: leadplant, wild indigo, partridge pea, silverleaf scurf pea, the white and purple prairie clovers, and purple vetch.

Between these two great families is a host of others: the wild roses, windflowers, butterfly milkweed, shooting star, blue-eyed grass and yellow stargrass—each representing a special tribe.

Many of the prairie's flowers ("forbs" to the botanist) are "decreasers" that cannot tolerate abuse by plow, cow, and mower. They tend to fade and fail in the course of agribusiness. Rugged and successful as they are in climax prairie, they may never survive intense land-use pressures—such as legumes that are avidly sought by livestock. Those plants may have withstood transient bison, but cannot live under the continuous trampling and overgrazing of most modern pastures.

Rarest of all prairie flowers are the orchids, especially the prairie white-fringed orchid—it may be

Phlox, paintbrush, and lousewort spangle Missouri's Coyne Prairie in early summer. Purchased in 1886 by Patrick Coyne with mustering-out pay from the Civil War, it never was plowed.

Long filaments that develop from the fruits of ripened flowers help give prairie smoke its name. When the wind blows through a field of these flowers, the resulting motion and color resembles drifting smoke. This flower was growing at the Conservancy's Crossman Prairie in Iowa.

several feet tall with a cluster of fringed white blooms with floral spurs over two inches long.

Found in boggy parts of the old prairie, it is the stoutest of our wild orchids, but one of the weakest survivors. Sought by people who try—rarely with any success—to transplant it in gardens, it also has a particularly weak link in its life cycle. At twilight its flowers have a delicate fragrance that brings the sphinx moth, said to be the only insect that can pollinate the plant. And so this once abundant, now rare orchid is beset by human enemies—not just those with spades or drainage schemes, but also the ones armed with pesticides. For as that special moth goes, so goes one of the wild prairie's most special flowers.

With frost, the show closes.

The rich and gaudy displays of floral elegance vanish, leaving only dried stalks and some frost-blighted seedheads and pods. The grasses make a final statement, an epilogue of golds, bronzes, and winey russets, and then the prairie sleeps.

The pendulum of annual flowering has swung to one limit but has already begun to swing back. In a few bleak months there will be pasqueflowers again.

One of the rarest of all: the western prairie fringed orchid at The Nature Conservancy's Pembina Trail Preserve in Minnesota.
The flower's rich fragrance draws its only pollinator, a sphynx moth. As pesticides kill the moth, the orchid dies as well.

"The Red Buffalo"

The aboriginal high-grass prairie is nearly gone now. And it was something else. When it burned, they say, it filled the sky with its smoke; the smoke blew through the forest belt, and when the Dakotah were rounding up the game, the Ottawa in the woods of Michigan smelt that great hunt in the air.

Donald Culross Peattie, A *Prairie Grove*

For a people with no written language, the first Americans certainly had a way with words.

They had a knack of giving natural events far more colorful names than anything white men could come up with. So when they observed wildfire devouring prairie like some elemental bison herd, certain Indians called it "The Red Buffalo."

The tallgrass country of that time was an immense reach of "warm season" grasses that were green and growing only in late spring and through summer. Come autumn, the life of the grasses retreated underground for the winter, leaving tinder-dry upper parts. Sooner or later, The Red Buffalo came there to feed.

Most of the fires that swept those grasslands were probably kindled by lightning strikes during thunderstorms. Other fires were set by the Indians themselves to drive game or simply improve pasturage, for they had learned that the new growth following a burn was highly palatable to bison and horses. Early settlers often ignited the prairie by accident with campfires, sparks from chimneys, or even the burning wadding of their shotguns.

Left: A stand of switchgrass on the Konza Prairie succumbs to the "red buffalo" with an almost explosive intensity.
Above: After a fire; a box turtle emerges from a muddy seep.

Lightning strikes the Flint Hills of Kansas. A prairie fire in the making?

Right: As violent and intense as a prairie fire may be, it does no harm to the grasses it consumes. Their growing points are safely underground.

Whatever the cause, one thing was certain: each spring and fall, somewhere in the prairielands, a billionweight of highly inflammable fuel would be set ablaze.

If there was no wind and the humidity was high, fire might move slowly across the prairies. But if there was wind and the grass was bone-dry, the prairie would be swept by fire blizzards with walls of flame thirty feet high, roaring over hundreds of square miles "as fast as a horse could run." This was one of the greatest terrors faced by isolated prairie settlers, and for good reason. Whole families, and even towns, perished in these stampedes of The Red Buffalo. In the dry autumn of 1885 the old war chief Sitting Bull counseled some South Dakota schoolchildren about escaping prairie fire: *Go to bare ground, or onto sand, gravel or plowing. Or set a backfire. Go to a place with no grass. But do not run!*

Yet even as he said that, the free-ranging Red Buffalo was on the verge of extinction. Plowed fields and tree claims were breaking the continuity of grassland; prairie

Above: In autumn, dry prairie grasses are an immense fuel load awaiting a spark. Without occasional fire, the heavy thatch of dead grasses can impede new growth.

Right: A wall of flame advances during a controlled burn at Konza Prairie. Fire is essential for maintaining the prairie landscape.

fires could no longer run freely.

Still, like the bison with which it had coexisted, The Red Buffalo never vanished entirely.

Its range has been greatly restricted, to be sure, but it still serves a purpose. Harnessed and controlled, it helps maintain the few scraps of true prairieland that still remain. For ruinous as fire may seem, it does little real damage to tallgrass prairie. By burning dead plant materials and unlocking their minerals for return to the soil, it feeds the next generation of grasses and flowers. The actual growing points of the grasses are safe underground and not harmed. Fire is also a first line of defense against the trees and shrubs that are always waiting to invade grasslands if given half a chance. All in all, it is a key factor in prairie ecology, and carefully calculated burning is the most useful tool in prairie management today.

And so The Red Buffalo that once terrified great-grandad has become a docile and subservient ox—but is still found in the remnants of its ancient pastures.

A Place of
Hope and Promise

Within the prairie the conditions of life are severe.... After thousands of years, the species

have adjusted to the environment. The plants, with few exceptions, are remarkably free from

disease, regardless of weather, and are little injured by high winds or extreme heat. They may

be harmed by late freezing or–infrequently–be stripped of their leaves and battered to the

ground by hail, but they rarely or never are killed. Those that were unfit have disappeared.

John Ernest Weaver, *Prairie Plants and Their Environment*

Few landscapes appear more lifeless and forbidding than a northern prairie in deep winter.

But don't believe everything you see.

I remember a late December afternoon in northern Iowa when I was hunting pheasants across open farmlands as hard and colorless as iron. All day I had labored through dreary fields of white, gray, and faded duns. The only flashes of real color had been a ringnecked rooster running on the snow ahead, and a red fox crossing a far hillside.

My homeward course took me across a quarter-section of native prairie that I had been saving for

Left: Cold, bleak, and lonely, perhaps, but the life forces of Konza Prairie, and all prairies, remain protected underground during the winter.
Above: Like the prairie that nurtures it, the bison is virtually winterproof.

last—a shaggy landscape as snow-choked and dead as the rest of the world. Then, up ahead in the gathering dusk, I could see Christmas lights in the window of a farmhouse, their colors glowing across the snow-crusted prairie, a beacon of light and warmth and people. It was a vivid contrast to the piece of Old Original in which I stood, a wild place that had never known the touch of man, nor any laughter or Christmas trees—nor any other kinds of trees, for that matter. The tallgrass prairie lay empty and featureless except for the broken grass stems that drew circles on the snow. I don't think I've ever had such a keen and poignant sense of being outside looking in, of being shut out from all joy and laughter, than on that darkling prairie.

If human loneliness can be defined as a bleak desolation of spirit—a sort of gray hopelessness unrelieved by any color or joy—then winter prairie on an overcast evening is surely one of its embodiments.

Yet I knew that was only illusion, for no place holds more life or promise than a patch of tallgrass prairie—even in the dead of winter. That grim place promised more life and color than any Christmas tree with gaudy lights. It had simply withdrawn, waiting.

Switchgrass, on hold for spring.

48

A prairie schoolhouse built of the same stone that underlies Kansas' Flint Hills. The school is an unused part of yesterday; the prairie on which it stands is a useful part of today and tomorrow.

Even in deep winter, some prairie animals remain active. Tracks reveal that meadow mice have come up from their nests to prospect among coneflower stems and icy grass.

No other community vanishes more completely in late fall. None returns more richly with the fine days of spring. Most of a true prairie's standing stock dies back each year; only the few woody shrubs survive above ground. The greater amount of life goes underground, into the deep and powerful banks of energy known as prairie loam. Somewhere under my feet in that barren place were the life forces of prairie orchids, butterfly milkweed, purple coneflower, the magenta torches of blazing star and the creamy blooms of wild indigo, and the lofty grasses that named such prairies. All would return, as they had each spring and summer for a hundred centuries.

There was other life as well.

Far out in the prairie I had cut the trail of a white-tailed jackrabbit. It had been loafing along, prospecting near a little thicket of wild plum, when its tracks suddenly lined out in a highly inspired way. Nearby was a line of coyote tracks that also showed a certain urgency. The race led off to the south and I was never able to determine the winner. But with that lightly crusted snow, I'd have bet on the jackrabbit.

There were deer mouse tracks everywhere between the tents of broken grasses. Under the snowcrust, down out of the wind, there would be a deep, snug thatch of grass culms and leaves with an intricate maze of byways and secret passages and nests, with a wealth of seeds and juicy, slumbering insects. I had seen no signs of any winged mouse-hunters that day, although the week before certain roadside fenceposts suddenly seemed to have grown tall caps of snow—and we knew that snowy owls had been driven far southward by lack of food in their northern ranges.

For all its apparent lifelessness, that scrap of native prairie was the most vital place in a sterile landscape of corn stubble and overgrazed pastures. Unlike those other places, the prairie was a magnet for native wildlife dispossessed by agribusiness. Its shelter didn't vanish each fall just as hard times were coming on; that bit of wild grassland was there as it had always been, a place of great antiquity and eternal youth.

Now I have to admit that a Christmas prairie lacks the appeal of a blazing Yule log or a bowl of eggnog.

A cottontail rabbit suns itself in midwinter.

Written on snow: the mingled tracks of meadow mice and a passing fox.

A bitterly cold winter night comes to an end at Konza Prairie. Extremes of temperature characterize prairie landscapes and help shape their ecology.

The cold solitude of it, especially in a wire-edged wind, can make even last-minute shopping look good.

But there's something there that I'd give a lot to see, and which I'll never find at any fireside or shopping mall: a snowy owl on the hunt for deer mice at night, floating silently over the prairie under a winter moon.

The thick fur of a red fox turns away the deepest cold—and adds a flash of color to an Iowa prairie.

The Far Edge

Of all things that live and grow upon this earth, grass is the most important.... From the first oak openings of Ohio and Kentucky till it washed to the foot of the Rockies, grass ocean filled the space under the sky. Steppe meadow, buffalo country, wide wilderness, where a man could call and call but there was nothing to send back an echo.

Donald Culross Peattie, *A Prairie Grove*

ON THE OSAGE

'Way down yonder in the Indian Nation,

Rode my pony on the reservation

In those Oklahoma Hills where I was born.

Woody Guthrie

It's "the black hole" to certain airline pilots on redeye flights. They would be far above northeastern Oklahoma, over rural landscapes where night was pierced by the lights of towns, farms, and traffic. Then suddenly, nothing. An unlit mysterious void. Hundreds of square miles of almost unrelieved darkness. The Black Hole.

To pilots on daytime runs, the reason is as clear as prairie air. There aren't any town lights because there aren't any towns. Or much in the way of traffic or rural dwellings, either. The settled Oklahoma farmlands to the east and west are suddenly diluted by broad sweeps of grassy space—the great unbroken roll of Oklahoma's Osage Hills, whose fertile soils are too thinly spread over flinty beds of limestone to take a plow.

This is the southerly end of a north-south landform that extends northward almost to the Nebraska line. In Kansas it is the "Flint Hills" or "Bluestem Hills"; in Oklahoma it's called "the Osage Hills" or simply "The Osage." In both states it is largely unplowed uplands

Left: The Nature Conservancy's Tallgrass Prairie Preserve.
Above: Bald eagles have been released in the Osage region
in an effort to restore them to the prairies.

that may not make corn or wheat, but are wonderfully adapted to grass and cattle—an enclave of boots and saddles in a realm of cornpickers and wheat combines. And because the native sods have never been broken for crops, these hills constitute the greatest reach of native tallgrass prairieland remaining in the New World.

It is not, however, genuine tallgrass prairie. Some of it may be again, but for now it's prairie pasture, grazed or mown short for the most part. And one of the fondest dreams of many people has been the restoration of a large block of The Osage to its original condition. Now, at last, it is hope susceptible of attainment.

In the grassy heart of The Osage, about twenty miles north of the town of Pawhuska, lies the 30,000-acre Barnard Ranch. It's an old outfit, and for the first time in about eighty years it is in new ownership: bought by The Nature Conservancy as the cornerstone of a major tallgrass prairie restoration. It is only the beginning. More will be added to the initial 30,000 acres, all of it restored and managed.

Why is the Conservancy undertaking a prairie restoration on such a large scale? Aren't there prairie

Black-eyed susans.

With time and effort, The Nature Conservancy's Tallgrass Prairie Preserve will bring back meadows like this: riots of spiderwort, black-eyed susans, Indian blanket, plains beebalm, and many other flowers.

One of the prime components of the prairie is sheer space. The Tallgrass Prairie Preserve
has plenty of that, decorated with plants such as these pale purple coneflowers.

preserves enough as it is? And why the Barnard Ranch?

Native tallgrass prairie is the rarest of all North America's major biomes. It's been said that of the original 142 million acres of "true prairie" only about ten percent remains, implying that there are still 14 million acres surviving. If there really is that much left (and it's doubtful), most of it is in scraps and odd fragments. Even if such bits and pieces have never been disturbed, that's not good enough. A real tallgrass prairie is more than just a plot of native grasses and forbs. It is a system defined by climate, weather, size, and the interaction of fire and grazing bison. And

because those factors no longer combine as a balanced whole anywhere in North America, true tallgrass prairie can be considered to be extinct as a natural, functioning ecosystem.

Late in 1988, The Nature Conservancy consulted national prairie authorities to consider the question of a major prairie preserve. Among other things, it was agreed that:

• a functioning tallgrass prairie system does not now exist,

• such a community must include reestablishment of the fire/bison interaction,

Trees mark water on the Tallgrass Prairie Preserve, which includes springs and streams in a self-contained watershed free of outside pollution.

• the best chances to do that are in the Flint Hills of Kansas or Oklahoma's Osage Hills,

• a prairie preserve should be in the most diverse landscape possible, including a complete watershed and a core of at least 16,500 acres in order to maintain a minimum viable bison population (500 breeding adults) in a fire/bison interaction.

All of these factors could be obtained at only one site—in the Osage Hills of northeastern Oklahoma, where the Barnard Ranch was for sale at a reasonable price. And so the Conservancy bought it.

It was a good buy. The big ranch has been well

The prairie soils of Kansas' Flint Hills and Oklahoma's Osage Hills are rich enough,
but flinty beds of limestone near the surface have prevented plowing.

Bison are an integral part of the long-term management plan for the Tallgrass Prairie Preserve. Along with fire, bison will be used to restore and maintain native prairie ecology.

managed through the decades, and its prairie base is in generally good shape. It may lack the shaggy, varied richness of the old original, perhaps, but it's not tame land. It is wild land needing only a chance to break free and reassert its old ways, and the Conservancy will be giving it that chance. That block of 30,000 acres is an ideal foundation for restoring a landscape that would not only be big enough to *look* like a prairie, but big enough to *act* like a prairie, supporting the kinds of prairie life it should.

It's a wonderfully diverse place, a varied prairiescape lying just beyond the western outriders of the Ozark forestlands. Along the easterly flanks of the Osage Hills are stunted forests of post oak and blackjack oak. Farther out, in the prairie creek valleys, there are likely to be groves of boxelder, ash, cottonwood, and hackberry. The creeks are unlike any I knew as a boy in Iowa, where our creeks cut into deep prairie soils. Those in The Osage cut no deeper than the limestone underpinnings, dancing over little waterfalls and bright riffles, through rock-walled pools and down runs that may be floored with bedrock pavements.

Each spring, greater prairie chickens perform mating displays on leks at the Tallgrass Prairie Preserve.

A restoration that approaches the original prairie condition won't be simple, quick, or cheap. The composition of plant species in The Osage has been altered by more than a century of ranching, and the resumption of old rhythms and balances will depend on judicious replacements—the vital bison/fire interaction—and time.

Those prairies are missing many of their original fauna, and some of their old-time flora. The cast of characters has been drastically altered. Yet the main stage is still there. Now it's a matter of casting, of organizing the *dramatis personae*, of lining up the permanent stage crew that will oversee the production. This critic predicts standing ovations from audiences who know high drama when they see it.

Once again, as so often in the past, The Nature Conservancy is the backer of a long-running hit.

Two male prairie chickens challenge each other in a courtship duel at the Tallgrass Prairie Preserve.

SOME PRAIRIE WATERS

...this is the land of marshes. Many are gone where man must live; but on an April morning one may stand on a prairie knoll with his feet in pasque flowers, his head in the heavens, and see before him myriads of wildfowl on marshes reaching beyond the horizon.

H. Albert Hochbaum, *The Canvasback On a Prairie Marsh*

When the last glacial advance shrank back to the Arctic after ravaging what is now north-central Iowa, most of Minnesota, and the eastern Dakotas, it left a geologic mess.

Sheets, ridges, and mounds of ground-up, heaved-up glacial junk were strewn over thousands of square miles—a rumpled landscape with a remarkable talent for trapping and holding surface waters. Lakes and ponds formed behind the damming of glacial moraines, in the oxbows of extinct Ice Age rivers, and in

"kettleholes" where ice blocks had been buried in glacial till. Millions of swales, hollows, and basins were filled with water and generally stayed that way.

It was a baby landscape from which standing waters could not easily escape. Today, more than 11,000 years later, its natural drainage systems are still immature. Seen from the air against low light, the ponds, marshes, and lakes are strewn like silver coins flung over a region that is often as much water as land. This is the fabled prairie pothole region, 300,000

Left: Prairie wetlands such as those on the Squaw Creek National Wildlife Refuge in Missouri may be the richest wetlands in the world. Above: Coreopsis grace a prairie swale near Lockwood, Missouri.

The prairie pothole region of the Dakotas is a maze of sloughs, ponds, and shallow lakes. These wetlands provide critical nesting areas and migration stopovers for a vast number of North America's ducks, geese, and swans.

square miles of wetlands in the northern Midwest and southern Canada.

A prairie "pothole" is a water-filled basin of glacial origin. It's usually round and usually small, but not necessarily either. Potholes come in a wild assortment of sizes and shapes, but all are alike in their lush aquatic vegetation and rich blooms of plankton and insect life. Blessed with warm summers, and cradled in fat prairie soils that have not yet had their treasure troves of nutrients leached away by drainage, such places are simmering kettles of life. They are among the most productive wild wetlands in the world.

A male ruddy duck in a prairie marsh.

The sub-humid climate of the pothole region not only built a deep grassland humus rich in nitrogen and phosphorous, charging the glacial wetlands with fertility, but created a prairie biome that is far more attractive to waterfowl than is forest. This is wildfowl country supreme. Each spring and fall sees the Grand Passage of wildfowl through the northern prairie wetlands: clouds of shorebirds, herons, swans, ducks, and geese that come there to breed, or stop over on their long migrations. Up to half of all the waterfowl produced in the United States may be raised in this prairie pothole country in some years.

Migrating monarch butterflies pause on goldenrod at Chiwaukee Prairie, 580 acres of the richest prairie in Wisconsin.

Native wild iris is nearly hidden in the ferns and sedges of a prairie swale.

Left: At the western edges of the tallgrass region, whooping cranes stop each spring and fall at such prairie wetlands as Kansas' Cheyenne Bottoms and Nebraska's Platte Prairie.

Like the wild grasslands in which they lay, most of those wetlands have been done in by agribusiness. The original 20 million acres of prairie wetlands in the United States have shrunk to about 7 million acres, and the hosts of attendant waterfowl have faded apace. Still, enough of each still remain to give a vision of the primeval abundance that existed there.

The marshes and potholes of the Upper Midwest are prairie classics of one kind.

Nebraska's Platte River is another.

It is the archetypal prairie stream. In spate it is a raging bull buffalo of a river, brown and powerful, bulling its way eastward to the wide Missouri. With its flooding spent, it becomes a cougar sort of river, lean and sinewy, muscled with sandbars and driftwood and drowsing in the sun.

In prairie parlance the Platte is a "braided river" with innumerable shoals and channels. A river of many parts, as all prairie rivers are. But the Platte has a part that is shared by no others: it is the preeminent sandhill crane river, a mile wide and an inch deep, and tall with birds.

In early March the river seems almost lifeless. The riparian groves of cottonwoods and willows are bleak and skeletal with no sounds but crow and wind and the whisper of water past the towheads in the channels.

Then, early one morning, a farmer walks into his barnyard and looks skyward. He throws his seed-company cap high into the air and yells: "They're back! The cranes are back!" The grip of winter has been broken. The promise of spring is now official.

Overnight the river is transformed by a rich infusion of life. The bare sandbars are suddenly clad with gray forests of lesser sandhill cranes. They are among the most ancient of birds, unchanged for millions of years. In flight, with wings spanning six feet, they are unmistakable. Egrets and herons fly with legs extended and necks curved back over their bodies. Flying cranes are like flung javelins, necks and legs fully extended, reaching hungrily for distance and capable of traveling 600 miles in a single day.

*The wide Missouri River is a flyway for millions of waterfowl
bound for the pothole region of the eastern Dakotas and beyond.*

Nebraska's Platte is a "braided" prairie river whose broad shallows and sandbars draw countless sandhill cranes in their spring migration.

Each night over a half-million of the stately birds roost in shoal waters and on the sandbars of the Platte. Each morning, as the first sun turns the river into beaten gold and the cranes cast shadows thirty yards long, the big birds head out into the feeder fields. At sunset they return to the river.

They enliven the Platte for about a month and then, come early April, the river is suddenly craneless. The birds must keep trysts on nesting grounds that may be as distant as eastern Siberia, and another year will pass before the river hosts the huge staging flocks again.

And so away. From the north comes the fading, unmistakable flight call—a trumpeting whinny out of a time when the prairies were young but cranes were already old.

INTO THE WEST

Gradually to the westward the proportion of forest to grassland diminished, until forests in any proper sense of the word gave way to almost uninterrupted grass covering.

James C. Malin, *The Grassland of North America*

On the west flank of Kansas' Flint Hills, a lone cottonwood stands at the far edge of the tallgrass prairie.

If trees could think (and ambulate) this one might consider pulling up roots and heading into the sunset. Cottonwoods have a westering itch if any trees have, and are scattered along watercourses and coulees all the way to the feet of the Rockies.

It's one of the few eastern trees that's ready, willing, and able to brave the Great Plains. Others had come out of the East into the tallgrass country: soft maples, oaks, hickories, basswoods, sycamores, and elms had managed to survive on floodplains and sheltered folds in the upland prairies. Some had gotten to the far limits of the tallgrass country and a few, like the green ash and boxelder, had even ventured out into the Great Plains.

But only the cottonwood made it from the Atlantic coast all the way through the great interior grasslands to the feet of the Rockies.

Back East it was never highly regarded. Other trees were at least as big, with far better woods and reputations. To be a cottonwood in an eastern forest was to be a ninety-foot weed.

But all that changed near the 100th Meridian where most eastern trees faded and failed, dying of wind, thirst, and general loneliness out along the buffalo rivers. There the cottonwood came into its own, not suffering by comparison with the lordly oaks, maples, chestnuts, and tulip trees of the eastern states. It was enough that it was simply a tree, thick-boled and broad-limbed, breaking the infinite sweep of sky and grass and signifying shade, firewood, and water in a land that was notably lacking in all three.

Left: A savanna of bur oaks at Wisconsin's Chiwaukee Prairie marks an eastern approach to the tallgrass prairie region.
Above: Snow-on-the-mountain.

A lone cottonwood stands at the far edge of the tallgrass country in the Flint Hills of Kansas.

If there was one tree symbolizing the great open grasslands of the West, this was it. Sometimes it was a loner, like this old Flint Hills sentinel. But often the cottonwoods gathered in gallery forests along such storied rivers as the Cheyenne, Platte, Powder, Smoky Hill, Cannonball, Knife, and Crazy Woman Creek. In summer, their shade and grassy understories might be sought by bison herds or encamped Indians. Mountain men carved pirogues from the thick trunks; the Plains tribes used the inner bark for winter horse feed; ranchers built corrals of cottonwood and hanged rustlers from cottonwood limbs. The cottonwood may have come all the way from the Atlantic seaboard, but it was The Western Tree of fact and fiction, if such can be said of any tree.

And so the tallgrass prairies had begun with one kind of savanna and ended with another.

At the easterly edges of the tallgrass country, "barrens" of bur oaks. At the westerly edges and far beyond, gallery forests of cottonwoods. The first had done its best to let in the sky; the other tried to close it out. Neither had fully succeeded—which is to say that neither had really failed.

The westernmost reach of the tallgrass country is Arapaho Prairie Preserve in Nebraska, whose main river is the beautiful Niobrara.

CONCLUSION

The prairie sings to me in the forenoon and I know in the night I rest easy
in the prairie arms, on the prairie heart.

Carl Sandburg, *Prairie*

ROLLING FORWARD

These plains...are yet in themselves not flat, but exhibit a gracefully waving surface....

It is that surface, which, in the expressive language of the country, is called rolling,

and which has been said to resemble the long, heavy swell of the ocean

when its waves are subsiding after the agitation of a storm.

Judge James Hall, *Plumbe's Sketches*

Some early settlers, as well as some of the very last, came into the tallgrass prairie abruptly with few interim stops between the Wooden Country of the East and the open lands of the Midwest.

In most cases, however, the first settlers "rolled forward" more gradually out of the Old States. They often stayed for a generation or two in the prairie savannas and "barrens" of Ohio, Indiana, and Kentucky before moving westward again, finally breaking out onto the broad grasslands of Illinois. In a sense, they served a sort of cultural apprenticeship—a process of

adaptation that helped fit them for life on the true prairie.

My great-grandfather Thomas Postgate was a classic example of the latter.

His own great-grandfather had come from England in about 1750, settling in Virginia where the family remained until after the Revolution. Then one branch of sons went a-westering up into Pennsylvania and over into Ohio, where great-grandad was born in 1833. When he was a small boy the family moved to eastern Illinois at the edge of the Grand Prairie. There he grew

Left: Fall color isn't just for trees. At Konza Prairie, the big bluestem and prairie dropseed grasses take on rich russets and bronzes of their own. Above: Rose gentian, Niawathe Prairie, Missouri.

Rockhill Prairie near Warsaw, Missouri, is a Conservancy preserve whose high quality makes up for small size. Active restoration is under way on three intact prairies totalling thirty-five acres.

up and married, and from there he rolled on westward.

In 1853, in a covered wagon with his wife and baby son, he crossed the Grand Prairie and the Mississippi into central Iowa, finally reaching the west bank of the Skunk River to claim land "'cordin' to wood 'n water." Forty acres of the claim were in a prairie grove—the "old home place down in the timber" with its sprawling log house, garden, livestock pens, and all the shelter, fuel, and building supplies that a settler could want. Beyond the grove's edge were his 120 acres of rich prairie, and when Tom Postgate stopped rolling forward, that bit of virgin grassland was rolled under by his breaking-plow.

But some things have a way of rolling back; within thirty miles of the old homestead, just west of the town of Prairie City, Iowa, 8,000 acres of prairieland are being restored as the Walnut Creek National Wildlife Refuge.

Today, I often think of great-grandad's quarter-section of old Iowa. He saw prairie as something to be broken for his children; I see it as something to be saved for mine.

So do a lot of other people. Each year more relicts of native prairie are rescued and restored to something of their pre-settlement condition, a searching-out of collectibles as rare as they are graceful. Of the original 142 million acres of tallgrass prairies that once covered our heartland, nearly all are gone. The "Prairie State" of Illinois has only one hundredth of one percent of its original grassland, and much the same is true of the entire Midwest. It is easier to find virgin groves of redwoods than virgin stands of tallgrass prairie.

Our friend Neil Diboll, who owns the Prairie Nursery near Westfield, Wisconsin, says the true prairie was hunted down like some kind of "wolf ecosystem"—persecuted not because of any threat, but because of its rich promise. Both wolves and prairies represented kinds of wilderness that were intolerable to our notions of getting ahead. Today we're not as sure of that kind of progress as we once were, and have begun to feel that such things as wolves and wildlands should be carried with us into tomorrow.

Beebalm and big bluestem at the Missouri Botanical Garden's Prairie Demonstration Area near St. Louis.

Fremont's leather flower—a non-climbing clematis found in glades, savannas, and mixed prairies in Kansas and Nebraska—was named for 1800s explorer John C. Fremont.

The rising surge of interest in North American prairie has occurred almost entirely since World War II. Before that there were some obscure prairie ecologists and even a few zealous "prairie fairies," but little concerted effort in preserving what was left or restoring what had been.

Since then, various public agencies have begun acquiring prairie remnants as state parks and preserves. Private groups began rolling prairie forward as well. Of those, none has been more diligent than The Nature Conservancy. Dedicated to the preservation of natural areas, the Conservancy got into the prairie game early on. One of the key figures was frail, elderly Katharine Ordway—"The Lady Who Saved the Prairies." From 1970 until her death ten years later, she supported Conservancy acquisition of tallgrass prairies in South Dakota, Minnesota, Nebraska, Kansas, and Missouri. In the beginning, efforts had concentrated on small prairie remnants. Kay Ordway helped buy more of those, but also backed the acquisition of the biggest prairie

Above: The way it was—and still is. The Conservancy's 7,800-acre Samuel H. Ordway Prairie Preserve in north-central South Dakota has a herd of 300 bison.

Right: The rich hillsides of Konza Prairie hold unusual flowers—including this variant of the purple coneflower that grows in a narrow band from the Flint Hills northward.

preserves of the time. The first were the Konza Prairie in Kansas' Flint Hills, an area that would eventually grow to fourteen square miles, and the Ordway Prairie in north-central South Dakota—7,500 acres that were part tallgrasses and part midgrasses, with 400 wetland areas. A few years later Kay Ordway underwrote land for Missouri's Prairie State Park, over 2,000 acres of grassy distance and uncluttered horizons comprising a prairie rich in birds and flowers.

Through all of this there was growing interest in some sort of national tallgrass prairie preserve. The Flint Hills of Kansas held the most promise. A massive north-south ridge extending from near the Nebraska line down into northeastern Oklahoma, it had been largely spared from plowing by layers of flinty limestone just beneath the prairie's surface. However, efforts to create a Tallgrass Prairie National Park had all died a-borning. In 1961 when Interior Secretary Stewart Udall visited the site by helicopter (having been assured that it was owned by a willing seller) he

Last of the day's light on the Conservancy's Tzi-Sho Prairie near Liberal, Missouri.

was met by armed ranchers who felt otherwise. A 1962 bill failed in a Senate subcommittee because of opposition from cattlemen. In 1971 the Department of Interior tried again, with support from the Kansas governor. This, too, failed.

A decade later, federal efforts had shifted farther south. This time there was even wider support for some sort of federal prairie preserve in the Osage Hills of northeastern Oklahoma, but once again political backing faded as landowners objected and members of the Osage Tribe expressed concern for their oil rights on some of the land under consideration.

And again The Nature Conservancy ventured where bureaucrats and politicos feared to tread. In the heart of Oklahoma's Osage Hills, about twelve miles north of the town of Pawhuska, the Conservancy bought the 30,000-acre Barnard Ranch. When fully restored it will be the largest block of true prairie in North America—a broad grassland spanning 8.5 miles from east to west, and nine miles north to south.

All the while, bits and pieces of prairie remnants are being found and rescued along old railroad rights-of-way, in pioneer cemeteries, and obscure fence corners. As interest has grown, individual landowners have gotten into the act, either protecting prairie

In a showy display seen only on quality prairies, a swallowtail butterfly pauses on blazing star at Niawathe Prairie, Missouri.

Rich, varied, and brimming with the prairie life force: a pothole lake in northeastern South Dakota.

remnants in their ownership or restoring parts of farmlands to prairie. They were also finding the value of native warm-season grasses for midsummer pasturage. More and more, householders are planting little patches of prairie grasses and forbs for fun and ornament. Private and public arboretums are establishing their prairies, as are some colleges, universities, and high schools.

In spite of such efforts, and all the ones to come, North America's tallgrass prairie can never again be the rich, functioning ecosystem that it once was. As a balanced whole, covering millions of acres in rich and varied complexity, it is extinct.

So why bother with prairie restoration at all?

Why not let the last prairie remnants slip away and have done with them and get on with work in the croplands that have replaced them?

One of the current buzzwords in the scientific community is "biodiversity." It is better explained by example than by definition—and there is no better example than a prairie being preserved or restored in an artificial monoculture of cash grain and livestock.

Biodiversity is rarely a fixed constant. Like "balance of nature," it is a constantly adjusting, shifting phenomenon that tends toward stability in the long run. Within a natural community, it is a reflection of the number of species of plants and animals; *stability* is the relative constancy in the abundance of those plants and animals. Tallgrass prairie demonstrates both.

The tallgrass prairie of the Midwest is a prime example of conversion of a highly diverse and stable system to monocultures whose stability depends on a lot of tender, loving care. The original prairie was a vastly complex meld of plants and animals that was nearly destroyed in favor of monocultures of small grains. The short-term gains are undeniable: immense production from rich prairie soils, efficiency in harvest, and high profits. Of course, all this costs a great deal in terms of labor, energy, fertilizers, pesticides, and even irrigation. Because of their low biodiversity and inherent instability, monocultures are ready victims for drought, flood, hail, disease, and insects—none of which greatly affected the original grasslands.

Black-eyed susans in the wind, Chiwaukee Prairie, Wisconsin.

Red-winged blackbird nest, Hoffman Prairie, Iowa.

Dragonfly (alias "devil's darning needle") at The Nature Conservancy's Niawathe Prairie in Missouri.

A clump of the bunch-forming prairie dropseed is set about with white sage and big bluestem at the Freda Haffner Kettlehole Preserve, Iowa.

Indians, explorers, and early pioneers hunted wild turkeys along tree-lined waterways on the tallgrass prairie. Here a gobbler performs a mating display at the Tallgrass Prairie Preserve, Oklahoma.

Native prairie, on the other hand, is wonderfully diverse and stable. The monocultures that replaced much of it are wonderful, too. Low in diversity and unstable they may be, but they do more to feed and clothe us than do prairies. We need them, of course. But we also need significant remnants of native biomes. When we simplify complex natural systems by reducing them to monocultures, we reduce our inherent biodiversity and make ourselves more vulnerable to the sort of boom-and-bust mechanics that will always threaten our croplands. Native prairie is the endpoint of eons of evolutionary testing that has done its own good job of genetic engineering.

Livestock managers are finding the great value of the prairie's "warm-season" grasses that remain green and growing through midsummer, providing forage at a time when such "cool-season" grasses as bluegrass and the bromes are dormant. Soil scientists are scarcely beginning to understand the infinitely complex interactions of micro-organisms and native plants that have built the richest soils in the world. More and more, medical research is turning its attention to the obscure native plants and the rich promise of the tallgrass prairie's pharmacopoeia.

The scientist in me believes that enough prairie must be rescued and restored to make research practical. The romantic in me believes it can give us a glimpse of the immense original wealth which we have capitalized—of how things were as we first saw them long ago, when we were land-hungry and a-westering.

Part of the prairie mystique is the pure Americana embodied in things that most people have never seen before, and will see nowhere else. Flowers with the old homespun names of rattlesnake master, blazing star, blacksamson, prairie smoke, compass plant, butterfly milkweed, wild indigo, windflower, kittentails, spiderwort, Culver's root, queen-of-the-prairie, blue-eyed-grass, shooting star, catchfly, and many others, all woven into the fabric of tall grasses in a pioneer quilt of form and color.

To addicted prairie-hunters, such stuff has high antique value. They would rather discover a scrap of original prairie in some neglected fence corner than find a Chippendale chair at a garage sale. Part of this appeal is the extreme rarity of such bits and pieces; part of it is the splash of varied form and color that such a place lends a landscape given over to corn and soybeans. Then, too, there is sympathy for an underdog landscape that has been overwhelmed by our blind chase after Progress.

A more immediate appeal of tallgrass prairie is the fact that it can be simulated on almost any scale, from a backyard flowerbed to many acres. For the gardener wanting something striking and colorful without the usual fertilizers, pesticides, and irrigation, a patch of prairie forbs and grasses is ideal. It is the most self-reliant of natural gardens, thriving in spite of drought or insects and fiercely intolerant of invading weeds. It can't survive plowing or constant close mowing, but it can endure stresses that tame, pampered ornamentals could never survive.

For some of us, the appeal of tallgrass prairie may lie in the fact that it's about as close to being a fountain of youth as anything we'll ever know.

Nebraska prairie-seed producer Jim Wilson once said that "there is a mysterious something about the

Wild shooting star at the Sheldon L. Cook Memorial Meadow near Lockwood, Missouri.

One of the classic signatures of tallgrass prairie is the richly red-orange butterfly milkweed, named for its attraction to many butterflies. It is a common summer bloom in the Flint Hills of Kansas and Oklahoma.

A whitetail fawn explores a field of pale purple coneflowers at a privately owned prairie in northeastern Missouri.

Left: Yellow lady slippers are surrounded by golden alexander, phlox, and shooting star on Crossman Prairie, Iowa.

A western meadowlark sings a prairie song much different from that of its eastern cousin.

native grasses—a power, a spirit that both stirs the soul and quiets it." Neil Diboll says much the same thing: "When I want to relax or think something over, I head to the prairie for inspiration and spiritual renewal. In summer, the wildflowers never cease to amaze me with their variety and intricacy. In fall and winter, the golds and auburns of the prairie grasses can warm up even the coldest day. When visitors come to our home, the first place they want to see is the prairie!"

Native prairie is old, old. It has existed since the stars sang together, yet stays as young as April. Nearly all of the flora are perennials. Each year its grasses and forbs renew themselves, flowering and fruiting and retreating for winter into the deep banks of fertility they have fostered, always returning in the spring.

Forests, of course, also have their cycle of death and rebirth, of dying and seeding and sprouting. But they never display the rich, summerlong bursts of renewal that prairies do. The annual blooming of tallgrass prairie is steady, varied, and faithful, coming on in changing waves of form and color throughout the growing year. It is a faithful renewal that can kindle the sense of wonder Rachel Carson believed to be "an unfailing antidote against the boredom and disenchantments of later years, the sterile preoccupation with things that are artificial, the alienation from the sources of our strength...."

Prairie rose.

Wood lilies, black-eyed susans, and prairie phlox in a setting of young bluestem, Steele Prairie, Iowa.

Tallgrass prairie, such as Missouri's Coyne Prairie shown here, provided more than rich panoramas of color, form, and space. It also built the richest soils in the world, and in that wealth lay its destruction. Too rich to last, original prairie is now the rarest of major North American biomes.

TALLGRASS
PARKS AND PRESERVES

TALLGRASS PRAIRIE SITES

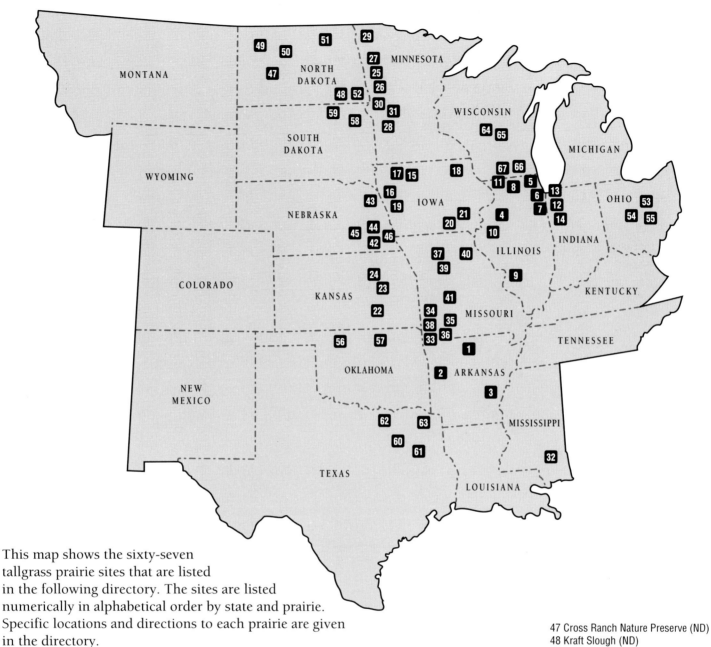

This map shows the sixty-seven
tallgrass prairie sites that are listed
in the following directory. The sites are listed
numerically in alphabetical order by state and prairie.
Specific locations and directions to each prairie are given
in the directory.

1 Baker Prairie (AR)
2 Cherokee Prairie National Area (AR)
3 Railroad Prairie State
   Natural Area (AR)
4 Goose Lake Prairie
   Nature Preserve (IL)
5 Illinois State Beach Park (IL)
6 Indian Boundary Prairie (IL)
7 Iroquois County
   Conservation Area (IL)
8 Nachusa Grasslands (IL)
9 Pere Marquette State Park (IL)
10 Reavis Hill Nature Preserve (IL)
11 Searls Park Prairie (IL)
12 Beaver Lake Nature Preserve (IN)
13 Hoosier Prairie Nature Preserve (IN)
14 Spinn Prairie Nature Preserve (IN)
15 Cayler Prairie (IA)

16 Five Ridge Prairie (IA)
17 Freda Haffner Kettlehole (IA)
18 Hayden Prairie (IA)
19 Kalsow Prairie (IA)
20 Rolling Thunder Prairie (IA)
21 Walnut Creek National
   Wildlife Refuge (IA)
22 El Dorado State Park (KA)
23 Flint Hills Drive (KA)
24 Konza Prairie (KA)
25 Agassiz Dunes (MN)
26 Blazing Star Prairie (MN)
27 Bluestem Prairie (MN)
28 Ordway Prairie (MN)
29 Pembina Trail Preserve &
   Pankratz Memorial Prairie (MN)
30 Richard and Mathilde Elliot
   Scientific & Natural Area (MN)

31 Staffanson Prairie (MN)
32 Harrell Prairie Hill Botanical Area(MS)
33 Diamond Grove Preserve (MO)
34 Marmaton Bottoms Prairie (MO)
35 Niawathe Prairie (MO)
36 Osage Prairie (MO)
37 Paint Brush Prairie (MO)
38 Prairie State Park (MO)
39 Taberville Prairie (MO)
40 Tucker Prairie (MO)
41 Wah-Kon-Tah Prairie (MO)
42 Burchard Lake Wildlife
   Management Area (NE)
43 Cuming City Cemetary Prairie (NE)
44 Nine-mile Prairie (NE)
45 Rock Creek Station (NE)
46 Twin Lakes Wildlife
   Management Area (NE)

47 Cross Ranch Nature Preserve (ND)
48 Kraft Slough (ND)
49 Lostwood National
   Wildlife Refuge (ND)
50 McHenry School Prairie (ND)
51 Shell Valley Prairie (ND)
52 Sheyenne National Grasslands (ND)
53 Bigelow Cemetery Preserve (OH)
54 Huffman Prairie (OH)
55 Smith Cemetery Prairie (OH)
56 Springer Prairie Preserve (OK)
57 Tallgrass Prairie (OK)
58 Crystal Springs Prairie (SD)
59 Samuel H. Ordway, Jr.
   Memorial Prairie (SD)
60 Clymer Meadow (TX)
61 County Line Prairie (TX)
62 Parkhill Prairie (TX)
63 Tridens Prairie (TX)
64 Avoca Prairie-Savanna (WI)
65 Black Earth Rettenmund Prairie (WI)
66 Chiwaukee Prairie (WI)
67 Kettle Moraine Fen and
   Low Prairie (WI)

TALLGRASS PRAIRIE DIRECTORY

Although extensive, this directory does not include all remaining areas of tallgrass prairie. Some locations have been excluded because of the delicate nature of their habitat, they are on privately owned land, or public visitation is not allowed. However, all major areas are listed here, and all sites are open to the public. Additional information can be obtained by calling the phone numbers listed for each site.

ARKANSAS

1. Baker Prairie

70 acres of tallgrass prairie in the Ozarks with the special attraction of grasshopper sparrow and rare plant species. Interpretive brochure and maps are available. In the town of Harrison off Goblin Drive. Owner: The Nature Conservancy and Arkansas Natural Heritage Commission. Contact: TNC (501) 372-2750, or Natural Heritage Commission (501) 324-9150.

2. Cherokee Prairie Natural Area

541-acre prairie that has never been plowed and still retains a full complement of native prairie grasses and wildflowers. 2 miles north of Charleston on Arkansas Hwy. 217. The prairie is on the west side of Arkansas 217 and the natural area is on both sides of Arkansas Hwy. 60. Owner: Arkansas Natural Heritage Commission. Contact: (501) 324-9150.

3. Railroad Prairie State Natural Area

257 acres of prairie occupying portions of the abandoned right-of-way of the former Chicago Rock Island and Pacific Railroad. Construction of a hard-surfaced, barrier free trail on the old railroad bed is scheduled for 1993. In Prairie and Lonoke counties between Carlise and DeValls Bluff, on the north side of U.S. Hwy. 70. Owner: Arkansas Natural Heritage Commission and The Nature Conservancy. Contact: Natural Heritage Commission (501) 324-9150 or TNC (501) 372-2750.

ILLINOIS

4. Goose Lake Prairie Nature Preserve

1,513 acres including dry-mesic, wet-mesic, and wet prairie, and prairie potholes. Interpretive center and trails. Southeast of Morris, north of Lorenzo Road, on Jugtown Road. Owner: Illinois Department of Conservation. Contact: IDOC (815) 942-2899.

5. Illinois State Beach Park

829 acres of wet to dry sand prairie on Lake Michigan. Interpretive center and trails. From Zion, take Sheridan Road south about 1 mile to Wadsworth Road. Go east to Illinois Beach State Park. Prairie on southern part of park. Owner: Illinois Department of Conservation. Contact: IDOC (708) 662-4828.

6. Indian Boundary Prairie

A 252-acre cluster of four prairies that are among the finest black soil prairies in the midwest. In Markham, east of Kedzie Ave., west of I-294, and between 155th and 157th streets. Owner: The Nature Conservancy, Northeastern Illinois University, and The National Land Institute. Contact: The Nature Conservancy (312) 346-8166.

7. Iroquois County Conservation Area

1,700 acres of wet to dry prairie and marsh. Parking provided. Northeast of Beaverville in southern and eastern parts of conservation area. Owner: Iroquoi Wildlife Area. Contact: (815) 435-2218.

8. Nachusa Grasslands

1,000-acre preserve. Home to endangered upland sandpipers, loggerhead shrikes, and many rare grassland animals such as badgers and short-eared owls. From Rochelle, take Illinois Hwy. 251 north to Flagg Road. Turn west onto Flagg Road and continue approximately 16 miles west to Lowden Road. Turn south onto Lowden Road and continue past Stone Barn Road. The preserve will be on your right. Owner: The Nature Conservancy. Contact: TNC (312) 346-8166.

9. Pere Marquette State Park

20 acres of loess hill prairie within the state park. Interpretive center and trails. West of Grafton on Illinois Hwy. 100. Owner: Illinois Department of Conservation. Contact: IDOC (618) 786-3323.

10. Reavis Hill Nature Preserve

454 acres of loess hill prairie. No staff on site. 5.5 miles south of Easton, 8 miles east of Kilbourne, south of County Highway 5. Owner: Illinois Department of Conservation. Contact: IDOC (309) 597-2212.

11. Searls Park Prairie

42 acres of wet to mesic prairie in the southeast corner of the park. Parking and trails. Northwest edge of Rockford on Central Avenue. Owner: Rockford Park District. Contact: (815) 987-8800.

**For more information on prairie sites in Illinois, call the Illinois Department of Conservation, Division of Natural Heritage at (217) 785-8774 or write to Lincoln Tower Plaza, 524 South Second Street, Springfield, Illinois 62701-1787.

INDIANA

12. Beaver Lake Nature Preserve

640-acre mixture of dry loose sand, wet depressions, and infertile flats. A refuge to many wildlife and plants native to prairies and wetlands. Go 3 miles north of Enos on U.S. 41, then east 1 mile, and north 1 mile. Permission to enter must be obtained from the Property Manager at LaSalle State Fish and Wildlife Area. Owner: Indiana Department of Natural Resources. Contact: LaSalle State Fish and Wildlife Area (219) 992-3019.

13. Hoosier Prairie Nature Preserve

439 acres of black oak savannas, mesic sand prairie openings, wet prairies, sedge meadows, and marshes. Plant diversity is high and native birds and other animals can be found. There is a 1-mile trail through the prairie. From U.S. 41 go east on Main Street toward Griffith. Parking lot is on right just after Kennedy Avenue. Owner: Indiana Department of Natural Resources, Division of Nature Preserves. Contact: Division of Nature Preserves (317) 232-4052.

14. Spinn Prairie Nature Preserve

29-acre remnant of tallgrass prairie community containing both mesic prairie and black and white oaks. From the U.S. Hwy. 421/Indiana Hwy. 24 intersection in Reynolds, go north on U.S. 421 for 2 miles. Turn right and go 0.2 mile to a "T", turn right. The prairie is on the right. Owner: The Nature Conservancy. Contact: TNC (317) 923-7547.

IOWA

15. Cayler Prairie

160 acres ranging from dry to wet prairie and marsh. 40 species of butterfly are found throughout the prairie. From Iowa Hwy. 86 and Iowa Hwy. 9 west of Spirit Lake, take Iowa 9 west for 3.5 miles. Turn south on gravel road for 2.5 miles. The preserve is on the east side of the road. Owner: Bureau of Preserves and Ecological Services. Contact: DNR (515) 281-8524.

16. Five Ridge Prairie

789 acres of dry prairie and woodland on steep wind-blown loess deposits. From Sioux City, take Iowa Hwy. 12 north to County Road K18. Turn northeast onto CR K18 and go approximately 3 miles north, until you are 0.3 miles south of CR C43. Turn west onto gravel road to preserve entrance. Owner: County Conservation Board. Contact: (712) 947-4270.

17. Freda Haffner Kettlehole

110 acres of dry mesic prairie, wetland, and hayfield. The two kettleholes on the preserve were formed when gravelly deposits settled around a large, isolated block of ice which broke off during a glacial advance about 14,000 years ago. Go west on Iowa Hwy. 86 from intersection with U.S. Hwy. 71 north of Milford. Continue west on gravel where County Road 32 turns north. Preserve is 2 miles west of Iowa 86 on north side of road. Owner: The Nature Conservancy. Contact: TNC (515) 244-5044.

18. Hayden Prairie

240 acres of mesic to wet prairie community, the largest black soil prairie in Iowa. From the intersection of Iowa Hwy. 9 and U.S. Hwy. 63 in Howard County, take Iowa 9 about 4 miles west, then north onto County Road V26. Continue north for 4.5 miles to the preserve. Owner: Iowa Department of Natural Resources, Bureau of Preserves and Ecological Resorces. Contact: DNR (515) 281-8524.

19. Kalsow Prairie

160 acres ranging from mesic prairie to wet prairie and pothole wetlands. Near the center of the buried Manson Crater, formed by meteor impact in pre-glacial times. From Iowa Hwy. 7 and County Road N65 in Manson, take CR N65 north for 4 miles. Turn west 1 mile to prairie. Owner: Iowa Department of Natural Resources, Bureau of Preserves and Ecological Services. Contact: DNR (515) 281-8524.

20. Rolling Thunder Prairie

123 acres of tallgrass prairie on a steeply rolling landscape. From U.S. Hwy. 69 and County Road G76 in Medora, in southern Warren County, take CR G76 west 3 miles to County Road R57. Turn north for 1 mile to the preserve on the west side of the road. Owner: Warren County Conservation Board. Contact: (515) 961-6169.

21. Walnut Creek National Wildlife Refuge

An 8,654-acre site is planned when this massive prairie restoration effort is completed in 1996. A visitor center is also planned, including an interpretive area with exhibits. There is a temporary visitor center that is currently open. From Iowa Hwy. 163 near Prairie City, turn south at Iowa Hwy. 117 onto County Road S6G for 2 miles. Turn west on South 96th Avenue West for 1 mile. Turn south on West 109th Street South for about 0.75 mile. The temporary office is on the east side of the road. Owner: U.S. Fish and Wildlife Services. Contact: (515) 994-2415.

**For more information on prairie sites in Iowa, call the Iowa Department of Natural Resources at (515) 281-5145 or write to Wallace State Office Building, East 9th and Grand, Des Moines, Iowa 50319-0034.

KANSAS

22. El Dorado State Park

8,000 acres total, much of which are prairie lands. The park has trails, camping facilities, prairie chicken observation, and more. Located just north and east of the city of El Dorado. Owner: U.S. Army Corps of Engineers. Contact: Kansas Department of Wildlife and Parks (316) 321-7180.

23. Flint Hills Drive

100 miles of scenic driving through tallgrass prairie lands. Begin the drive at Manhattan on Kansas Hwy. K177. Continue down through Council Grove and Cottonwood Falls to El Dorado. Owner: All off-road land is privately owned.

24. Konza Prairie

8,616 acres of tallgrass prairie including a nature trail. Managed by Kansas State University - Division of Biology. Located south of Manhattan, take exit 307 off I-70 and travel north and east on McDowell Creek Road for 4 miles. Turn onto gravel road marked with sign and drive to parking lot. Owner: The Nature Conservancy. Contact: TNC (913) 272-5115.

MINNESOTA

25. Agassiz Dunes

674.40 acres in a large dune field associated with Glacial Lake Agassiz. From Fertile, go south on state Minnesota Hwy. 32. After crossing the Sand Hill River, go 0.5 mile and turn right onto a gravel road. Go 0.5 mile and turn left onto a dirt road leading to a parking area. Owner: The Nature Conservancy. Contact: TNC (612) 331-0750.

26. Blazing Star Prairie

160 acres dominated by porcupine grass and numerous flowering plants that attract butterflies. Common animal life in the area includes white-tailed jack rabbit, greater prairie chicken, marbled godwit, Baird's sparrow, chestnut-collared longspur, and Sprague's pipit. From Felton, drive 4.3 miles east on County Road 34. Turn right onto an improved township line road and go south 1 mile to prairie. Owner: The Nature Conservancy. Contact: TNC (612) 331-0750.

27. Bluestem Prairie

3,258 acres within the range of the greater prairie chicken.

Protecting at least 307 native plant species, including 54 native prairie grasses. From Glyndon, go east on U.S. Hwy. 10 for 3 miles. Turn right onto Minn. Hwy. 9 and go 1.5 miles. Turn left onto a gravel road. This will transect the preserve. Park on north side of road. Contact: TNC (612) 331-0750.

28. Ordway Prairie

580.9 acres including an oak grove and aspen thickets. From Brooten, drive east on County Hwy. 8 for about 7 miles. Turn left onto Minnesota Hwy. 104 and travel south 3 miles to the northwest corner of the preserve. Owner: The Nature Conservancy. Contact: TNC (612) 331-0750.

29. Pembina Trail Preserve and Pankratz Memorial Prairie

Pembina-1935 acres, Pankratz-637 acres. Both preserves are examples of a vegetation community known as aspen parkland. Together they provide habitat for more than 60 species of birds. To reach Pembina, go east on County Road 45 in Harold from the intersection at Minnesota Hwy. 102 for about 6.3 miles. The preserve is on the right and marked with TNC signs. To reach Pankratz from here, continue west on County Road 45. Turn right and head north on County Road 46 to the preserve. It is also posted with TNC signs. Owner:The Nature Conservancy. Contact: TNC (612) 331-0750.

30. Richard and Mathilde Elliott
Scientific and Natural Area

529 acres of mesic and wet tallgrass prairie in the heart of the greater prairie chicken range. Observed species include 120 vascular plants, 19 butterflies, 2 amphibians, 1 reptile, 28 birds, and 9 mammals. From Lawndale, go north 2.5 miles on Minnesota Hwy. 52 to County Road 188. Turn right and go 1 mile to the preserve. Signs are posted. Owner: The Nature Conservancy. Contact: TNC (612) 331-0750.

31. Staffanson Prairie

95 acres including everything from open water to mesic prairie. On Minn. Hwy. 55 near Kensington, go northwest for about 2 miles. Turn right onto a gravel road and go about 0.5 mile to "T" intersection. Turn left and go 0.25 mile, turn right and go 1 mile to an easement road on the left. Owner: The Nature Conservancy. Contact: TNC (612) 331-0750.

MISSISSIPPI

32. Harrell Prairie Hill Botanical Area

150 acres of natural grasses surrounded by forest. From Forest, take Mississippi Hwy. 501 south 1 mile to Forest Road 518. Harrell Hill lies 2 miles east along FR 518, and signs mark the area. Owner: Mississippi Forest Service. Contact: (601) 469-3811.

MISSOURI

33. Diamond Grove Preserve

570 acres of prairie on cherty soils in southwest Missouri with a rich display of spring wildflowers. 4 miles west of Diamond Grove on Missouri Hwy. V, then 1.5 miles north on unpaved county road. Owner: Missouri Department of Conservation. Contact: (314) 751-4115.

34. Marmaton Bottoms Prairie

609 acres of bottom and wet prairie and a mix of wet-mesic savanna and bottomland forest. This is the largest unplowed wet prairie in Missouri. In Vernon County, 3 miles northwest of Nevada. Owner: The Nature Conservancy. Contact: TNC (314) 968-1105.

35. Niawathe Prairie

320 acres rich in flora, making this a showy prairie in spring and early summer. 8 miles north of Lockwood, 3.25 miles east of Sylvania. Owner: Missouri Department of Conservation and The Nature Conservancy. Contact: Missouri Department of Conservation (314) 751-4115 or TNC (314) 968-1105.

36. Osage Prairie

1,467 acres containing diverse flora and fauna, including prairie chicken and white-tailed deer. 6 miles south of Nevada on U.S. Hwy. 71, 0.5 mile west and 0.5 mile south on gravel road. Owner: Missouri Department of Conservation and The Nature Conservancy. Contact: Missouri Department of Conservation (314) 751-4115 or TNC (314) 968-1105.

37. Paint Brush Prairie

234 acres of upland prairie over soils formed from cherty limestone and shale, with showy flowers in the spring. In Pettis County, 9 miles south of Sedalia on east side of Missouri Hwy. 65. Owner: Missouri Department of Conservation. Contact: (314) 751-4115.

38. Prairie State Park

2,982 acres of rolling upland prairie over sandy and silt loam soils derived from shale and sandstone. Home to coyote, deer, prairie chicken, and northern harrier. Trails, guidebook, and nature center on site. 3 miles west of Liberal on County Hwys. K & P, 1 mile south on gravel road. Owner: The Missouri Department of Natural Resources. Contact: Missouri Department of Conservation (417) 843-6711.

39. Taberville Prairie

1,680 acres with some 400 plant species recorded and a permanent flock of prairie chickens. 0.5 mile east of Appleton City on Missouri Hwy. 52, 2 miles south on County Hwy. A, 7 miles south on County Hwy. H. Owner: Missouri Department of Conservation. Contact: (314) 751-4115.

40. Tucker Prairie

146 acres of flat, upland prairie over silt loam soils derived from loess. Some 224 plant species and varieties recorded for the area. 2.5 miles west of junction of I-70 and U.S. Hwy. 54. Owner: University of Missouri. Contact: Univ. of MO Columbia (314) 882-7541.

41. Wah-Kon-Tah Prairie

1,040 acres containing three permanent springs and several woody draws among the prairie soil. Large expanses of prairie on rolling terrain provide spectacular vistas of Missouri's prairie landscape. Prairie chickens, deer, and wild turkey can be found here. 2.5 miles northeast of El Dorado Springs on north side of Missouri Hwy. 82. Owner: The Nature Conservancy. Contact: TNC (314) 968-1105.

**For more information on more prairie sites in Missouri, call the Missouri Department of Conservation at (314) 751-4115, or write to P.O. Box 180, Jefferson City, Missouri 65102.

Nebraska

42. Burchard Lake Wildlife Management Area

560 acres of tallgrass prairie with prairie chicken booming grounds. 3 miles east and 1 mile north of Burchard in Pawnee County. Owner: Nebraska Game and Parks Commission. Contact: (402) 471-0641.

43. Cuming City Cemetery Prairie

11 acres of tallgrass with a variety of wildflowers. Take U.S. Hwy. 75 north of Omaha through Blair. Go 3.5 miles north of Blair, just past the airport/golf course. Turn west on the county road that crosses U.S. 75. The prairie is on the south side of the road, approximately 0.10 mile from the intersection. Owner: Dana College. Contact: (402) 426-9000.

44. Nine-mile Prairie

260 acres of tallgrass prairie, a classic research site of J.E. Weaver, Nebraska ecologist. Located on the outskirts of Lincoln on West Fletcher Avenue, 1 mile west of NW 48th Street. Owner: University of Nebraska Foundation. Contact: U. of Nebraska (402) 472-2971.

45. Rock Creek Station

Over 500 acres of tallgrass prairie and wooded ravines with an interpretive center and visible Oregon Trail wagon wheel ruts. Take Nebraska Hwy. 8 to Endicott. The station is 2.75 miles north, then 1 mile east. Owner: Nebraska Game and Parks Commission. Contact: (402) 729-5777.

46. Twin Lakes Wildlife Management Area

1,370 acres consisting of mostly native prairie land. 1 mile north of I-80, take Pleasant Dale interchange. Owner: Nebraska Game and Parks Commission. Contact: (402) 471-0641.

North Dakota

47. Cross Ranch Nature Preserve

6,000 acres of rolling mixed grass prairie and lush floodplain. A self-guided interpretive trail is open during the summer, and a bison herd can be seen from the Cottonwood Trail. Additional activities are available through the connecting Cross Ranch State Park. Near Bismarck. Owner: The Nature Conservancy. Contact: TNC-Cross Ranch Nature Preserve (701) 794-8741.

48. Kraft Slough

1,310 acres of tallgrass prairie with some of North Dakota's rare animals including swamp sparrow, and rare plants including dwarf spikerush and small yellow lady's slipper. 4 miles south, 2 miles east of Crete. Owner: Bureau of Reclamation. Contact: North Dakota Natural Heritage Inventory Program (701) 224-4892.

49. Lostwood National Wildlife Refuge

26,900 acres of mixed grass prairie including some of North Dakota's rare animals such as red-necked grebes, white-winged scooter, Cooper's hawk, whooping crane, piping plover, common tern, long-eared owl, Sprague's pipit, Baird's sparrow, and pygmy shrew. 20 miles north of Stanley on North Dakota Hwy. 8. Owner: U.S. Fish and Wildlife Service. Contact: North Dakota Natural Heritage Inventory Program (701) 224-4892.

50. McHenry School Prairie

130 acres of tallgrass prairie, home to Sprague's pipit, one of North Dakota's rare birds. 6 miles north and 4 miles east of Towner. Owner: North Dakota State Land Department. Contact: North Dakota Natural Heritage Inventory Program (701) 224-4892.

51. Shell Valley Prairie

60 acres of natural fen community with drooping locoweed, bog willow, and white lady's slipper. 10 miles north of Rolette, or 9 miles east of Dunseith. Owner: privately owned. Contact: North Dakota Natural Heritage Inventory Program (701) 224-4892.

52. Sheyenne National Grasslands

71,000 acres of sandhills tallgrass prairie, oak savanna, and hardwood forest. Site of numerous state rare plants and the federally threatened western prairie fringed orchid. A 25-mile portion of the North Country National Scenic Trail crosses through the grasslands. Southeastern North Dakota, east of Lisbon. Owner: U.S. Forest Service. Contact: U.S. Forest Service (701) 683-4342.

**For more information about prairie sites in North Dakota, call the North Dakota Parks and Tourism Department at (701) 224-2525, or write to the Parks & Outdoor Recreation Sites Division, Liberty Memorial Building-604 E. Boulevard, Bismarck, North Dakota 58505.

Ohio

53. Bigelow Cemetery Preserve

0.5-acre state nature preserve. Royal catchfly bloom here. 8 miles west of Plain City, off Ohio Hwy. 161. One mile south on Rosedale Road. Owner: Pike Township Trustees. Contact: Ohio Department of Natural Areas and Preserves (614) 265-6463.

54. Huffman Prairie

109 acres of mostly big bluestem, Indian grass, oxeye, and gray-headed coneflower. The Wright brothers took their first practice flight here in the early 1900s. Take I-675 south to Dayton-Yellow Springs Road. Exit and turn left into Fairborn, go to Ohio Hwy. 444 and turn right. Follow Ohio 444 to Gate 8c and enter base. Follow TNC signs. Owner: Department of Defense - Wright-Patterson Air Force Base. Contact: (513) 257-5535.

55. Smith Cemetery Prairie

0.6 acres of original prairie sod supporting relics of the original prairie grasses and wildflowers, especially big bluestem. Take Ohio Hwy. 161 west from Plain City. Turn south on Kramer/Chapel Road, then go west on Boyd Road. The preserve is on the north side. Owner: Darby Township Trustees. Contact: Ohio Department of Natural Resources, Division of Natural Areas and Preserves (614) 265-6463.

Oklahoma

56. Springer Prairie Preserve

40 acres of tallgrass prairie, mostly bluestem/switchgrass prairie. Home to short-eared owls, badgers, and jackrabbits.

Located approximately 17 miles north and 14 miles east of Enid. The preserve is fenced with a locked gate. Owner: The Nature Conservancy. Contact: Oklahoma State University, Dr. James McPhearson (405) 744-9560.

57. Tallgrass Prairie
32,000 acres of tallgrass prairie where fire and bison are being used to recreate a functioning tallgrass prairie ecosystem. The preserve includes self-guided nature trails, a 50-mile scenic drive on gravel roads, and free-ranging cattle and (by October 1993) bison. From Tulsa, take U.S. Hwy. 75 north to northwest Oklahoma Hwy. 11 to Pawhuska. Go north on Osage Avenue and follow signs to the preserve. Owner: The Nature Conservancy. Contact: (918) 287-4803.

SOUTH DAKOTA

58. Crystal Springs Prairie
1,920 acres of tallgrass prairie with at least 10 rare plant species, 2 rare butterfly species, 2 rare fish species, and calcareous fens. Travel 1 mile north from the town of Clear Lake, turn right at the rodeo sign, travel 3 miles east on Duel County 7, 1 mile north, 1 mile east, 1 mile north, then finally 1 and 1.5 miles east to the parking area on the south side of the road. Owner: Ducks Unlimited. Contact: The Nature Conservancy Dakota's Field Office (701) 222-8464.

59. Samuel H. Ordway, Jr. Memorial Prairie Preserve
This 7,800-acre pothole prairie on the Coteau is primarily mixed grass prairie that is dotted with big bluestem and prairie cordgrass around the 300-400 potholes. The hillsides are full of wildflowers in the spring and summer. The prairie also contains self-guided nature trails, teepee rings, and grazing bison. Located 8 miles west of Leola on South Dakota Hwy. 10. Owner: The Nature Conservancy. Contact: The Nature Conservancy Dakota's Field Office (701) 222-8464.

TEXAS

60. Clymer Meadow
311 acres making this the largest and highest quality example of blackland prairie remaining in Texas. From Celeste, take FM 1562 west about 2.3 miles. Turn north on County Road 1140 just before the large cylindrical tank. Go 0.8 mile and turn left at the first driveway on the left. Owner: The Nature Conservancy of Texas. Contact: TNC of Texas (210) 224-8774.

61. County Line Prairie
40 acres of blackland prairie. From Celeste, take FM 1562 for about 3 miles. Turn south on FM 36 (Merit Road) and go about 3 miles. Take the second dirt road west, then the first dirt road south, this follows the county line. The preserve is at the base of the hill on the left side of the road. Owner: The Nature Conservancy of Texas. Contact: TNC of Texas (210) 224-8774.

62. Parkhill Prairie
436 acres featuring a 52-acre relic of blackland tallgrass prairie and a vast array of colorful wildflowers. Walking trail. From Dallas, take the Central Expressway north for 30 miles to McKinney, exit onto U.S. Hwy. 380 east for about 15 miles to Farmersville. Take Texas Hwy. 78 north for about 10 miles

to FM 981 in Blue Ridge. Turn east at County Road 669, then left at CR 668. The prairie is on the north side of the road. Owner: Collin County. Contact: (214) 548-4619.

63. Tridens Prairie
97 acres of undisturbed blackland prairie. Over 150 grasses and wildflowers have been identified here. In Lamar County, 8 miles west of Paris on U.S. 82 at intersection FM 38. Owner: The Nature Conservancy of Texas and Texas Garden Clubs, Inc. Contact: The Nature Conservancy of Texas (210) 224-8774.

WISCONSIN

64. Avoca Prairie-Savanna
1,885 acres dominated by little bluestem, northern dropseed, and Junegrass. Open for group use, research, and individual nature study. From Avoca, take Wisconsin Hwy. 133 east 1.5 miles. Turn north on Hay Lane Road. Follow road beyond Marsh Creek 0.3 mile to parking lot. Owner: Wisconsin Department of Natural Resources. Contact: Wisconsin Bureau of Endangered Resources (608) 266-7012.

65. Black Earth Rettenmund Prairie
16 acres of dry-mesic prairie with more than 80 different plant species. From Black Earth, travel west on CTY KP (off Wisconsin Hwy. 78) for 1 mile. Then go south on CTY F for 0.25 mile to Fesenfeld Road and turn right. Park along road, but keep at least 4 feet from the edge of road. Owner: The Nature Conservancy. Contact: TNC (608) 251-8140.

66. Chiwaukee Prairie
580 acres of the richest known prairie in Wisconsin. Home to more than 400 native plant species and a variety of wildlife including kit fox, white-tailed deer, raccoon, ground squirrel, woodchuck, and at least 76 bird species. Open for hiking and observation. From I-94 between Kenosha and the Illinois state line, drive east on Wisconsin Hwy. 165 for about 6 miles. Turn right on Wisconsin Hwy. 32 (Sheridan Road) for about 1 mile. Turn left on 116th st. (Tobin Road) for 1 mile. Turn right on First Court (Marina Road). Travel 5 blocks to 121st street and turn right. Go 1 block to Second Avenue and turn right. Continue on to 119th st. Owner: The Nature Conservancy, University of Wisconsin - Parkside, and Wisconsin Department of Natural Resources. Contact: TNC (608) 251-8140.

67. Kettle Moraine Fen and Low Prairie
250 acres of fen and wet prairie, wet-mesic and dry-mesic prairie, southern edgemeadow, and oak openings. Open for group use, research, and individual nature study. From Eagle, go north 2.25 miles on Wisconsin Hwy. 67 to gated access road. Follow land 0.5 mile west to the site. Owner: Bureau of Endangered Resources, Wisconsin Department of Natural Resources. Contact: DNR (608) 266-7012.

Selected Bibliography

Allen, Durward. 1967. *Life of the Prairies and Plains.* New York: McGraw-Hill.

Blair, William D. Jr. 1989. *Katharine Ordway—The Lady Who Saved the Prairies.* Washington, D.C.: The Nature Conservancy.

Brown, Lauren. 1985. *Grasslands.* (An Audubon Society Nature Guide.) New York: Alfred A. Knopf.

Collins, Scott L. and Linda L. Wallace (eds.) 1990. *Fire in North American Tallgrass Prairies.* Norman: University of Oklahoma Press.

Costello, David F. 1969. *The Prairie World.* New York: Thomas Y. Crowell.

Curtis, John T. 1959. *The Vegetation of Wisconsin.* Madison: Univ. of Wisconsin Press.

Dondore, Dorothy Anne. 1961. *The Prairie and the Making of Middle America—Four Centuries of Description.* New York: Antiquarian Press.

Gregg, Joshia. 1967. *The Commerce of the Prairies.* Lincoln: Univ. of Nebraska Press.

Johnson, James R. and James T. Nichols. 1982. *Plants of the South Dakota Grasslands—A Photographic Study.* Bulletin 566, Agricultural Experiment Station. Brookings: South Dakota State Univ.

Kindscher, Kelly. 1992. *Medicinal Plants of the Prairie, An Ethnobotanical Guide.* Lawrence: Univ. of Kansas Press.

Kucera, Clair L. 1961. *The Grasses of Missouri.* Columbia: Univ. of Missouri Press.

MacBride, Thomas. 1926. *Landscapes of Early Iowa.* Iowa City: *The Palimpsest,* Iowa Historical Society.

Madson, John. 1982. *Where the Sky Began.* Boston: Houghton Mifflin.

Malin, James C. 1967. *The Grassland of North America Prolegomena to Its History.* Gloucester, Mass: Peter Smith.

McFarland, Julian E. 1969. *The Pioneer Era on the Iowa Prairies.* Lake Mills, Iowa: Graphic Publishing Co.

Peattie, Donald Culross. 1938. *A Prairie Grove.* New York: The Literary Guild of America.

Phillips Petroleum Company. 1963. *Pasture and Range Plants.* Bartlesville, OK.

Poggi, Edith M. 1934. The Prairie Province of Illinois—A Study of Human Adjustment to the Natural Environment. *Illinois Studies in the Social Sciences,* Vol. 19, No.3. Urbana: Univ. of Illinois.

Quick, Herbert. 1925. *One Man's Life.* Indianapolis: Bobbs-Merrill.

Reichman, O.J. 1987. *Konza Prairie—A Tallgrass Natural History.* Lawrence: Univ. of Kansas Press.

Rickett, Harold Williams. 1965. *Wild Flowers of the United States,* Vol. 1, parts 1-2. New York: McGraw-Hill.

Rolvaag, O.E. 1927. *Giants in the Earth.* New York: Harper & Brothers.

Runkel, Sylvan T. and Dean M. Roosa. 1989. *Wildflowers of the Tallgrass Prairie.* Ames: Iowa State Univ. Press.

Schwartz, Charles W. 1944. *The Prairie Chicken in Missouri.* Columbia: Univ. of Missouri Press.

Sears, Paul B. 1969. *Lands Beyond the Forest.* New York: Prentiss-Hall.

Steyermark, Julian A. 1963. *Flora of Missouri.* Ames: Iowa State Univ. Press.

Tobey, Ronald C. 1981. *Saving the Prairies—The Life Cycle of the Founding School of American Plant Ecology, 1895-1955.* Berkeley: Univ. of Calif.

Transeau, Edgar Nelson. 1935. "The Prairie Peninsula." *Ecology,* Vol. 16, No.3.

Weaver, J. E. 1954. *North American Prairie.* Lincoln, NE: Johnsen Publishing Co.

_____1968. *Prairie Plants and Their Environment: a 50-year Study in the Midwest.* Lincoln: Univ. of Nebraska Press.

_____and T. J. Fitzpatrick. 1934. *The Prairie.* Reprinted in 1980 by Prairie-Plains Institute of Nebraska, Aurora.

ABOUT THE AUTHOR

Iowa native John Madson has written extensively about the wildlife and natural history of prairies, plains, and rivers, as well as the life histories of many American birds and mammals. He is the author of such books as *Out Home*, *Stories From Under the Sky*, *Where the Sky Began*, and *Up On the River.* He has also contributed to many other books, including *Words From the Land*, *Audubon Wildlife Treasury*, and *Carl Sandburg's Illinois*. He lives in Godfrey, Illinois, with his wife and family.

ABOUT THE PHOTOGRAPHER

Frank Oberle first became interested in prairiescapes while photographing the Falcon Press book, *Missouri On My Mind*. An accomplished photographer of wildlife and nature, his photographs have appeared in *National Geographic*, *Audubon*, *Life*, and many other books and calendars. He lives in St. Louis, Missouri, with his wife, and recently purchased a farm with 200 acres of unplowed prairieland.

ABOUT FALCON PRESS

Falcon Press publishes a wide variety of high quality books and calendars, specializing in titles for people who love wildlife, wild places, and outdoor recreation.

Our FalconGuide series features state-by-state guides to hiking, wildlife viewing, river floating, rockhounding, and scenic drives. We proudly publish The Nature Conservancy's yearly wall and desk calendars.

To purchase our titles, contact your local bookstore, or call our toll-free number, 1-800-582-2665. A free catalog describing all our books, calendars and posters may be obtained by calling or writing Falcon Press Publishing Co., Inc., P.O. Box 1718, Helena, MT 59624.

About The Nature Conservancy

The mission of The Nature Conservancy is to preserve plants, animals, and natural communities that represent the diversity of life on Earth by protecting the lands and waters they need to survive.

To date the Conservancy and its members have been responsible for the protection of more than 6.4 million acres in 50 states and Canada. It has helped like-minded partner organizations to preserve millions of acres in Latin America and the Caribbean. While some Conservancy-acquired areas are transferred for management to other conservation groups, both public and private, the Conservancy owns more than 1,300 preserves—the largest private system of nature sanctuaries in the world.

The Conservancy has at least one field office in every state and its members number more than 700,000. Members receive the Conservancy's bimonthly membership magazine, a newsletter from the nearest office, and information about volunteer opportunities. To learn more about membership, call 1-800-628-6860, or write The Nature Conservancy, 1815 North Lynn Street, Arlington, Virginia 22209.